MW00442581

THE MOST PRODUCTIVE PEOPLE IN HISTORY

THE MOST PRODUCTIVE PEOPLE IN HISTORY

18 Extraordinarily Prolific Inventors, Artists and Entrepreneurs, From Archimedes to Elon Musk

MICHAEL RANK

Five Minute Books

A Fevkalade Publishing Company · Kansas City

Copyright © 2015 by Michael Rank

Requests for permission to reproduce material should be sent to Permissions, Five Minute Books
Published by Five Minute Books, 12604 Barkley St. Kansas City, MO 62209

http://michaelrank.net

All Rights Reserved

Rank, Michael M.

The most productive people in history: 18 extraordinarily prolific inventors, artist, and entrepreneurs, from Archimedes to Elon Musk / Michael Rank.

Summary: " Greek scientist Archimedes discovered mathematical phenomena that weren't confirmed for 17 centuries. He also single-handedly defended Syracuse from the Romans by building massive catapults, a huge iron claw that could pick ships up out of the ocean, and even a solar-powered death ray. Ibn Sina was a medieval mathematician who wrote hundreds of treatises, including a medical compendium used in European universities for the next 400 years. Isaac Newton invented classical physics and was one of the inventors of calculus. Theodore Roosevelt won the presidency twice, was the first American to earn a belt in judo, hunted, wrote numerous books, and read four hours a day even during the busiest moments of his political life. This book will explore the lives of the 18 most productive people in history. We will look at their biographies, understand the cultural context into which they were born, and see the methods that they used to achieve such sweeping results. Perhaps with their examples in mind, we can create enough time to focus on the tasks in life that are truly meaningful." – Provided by publisher.

Includes bibliographical references.

ISBN: 1511671343
ISBN-13: 978-1511671347

Printed on acid-free paper.

Printed in the United States of America.

ACKNLOWLEDGMENTS

This book could not have existed in its current form without the input of many wonderful people. They offered critical feedback in the early stages of this project, particularly in sharpening the good sections and omitting the dull ones. I apologize in advance for any omissions.

To early readers Robert Barnhouse, Joe Fegan, Clifton McLendon, Nancy Taylor, Rodrigo Petters, Stephen Lowien, and Jack Lusk: I couldn't have caught all the things I missed without you, nor would I have realized which parts to expand and which parts to contract. Particular thanks to Thomas Boullion, whose excellent commentary helped me feel as though I were writing to one reader.

Thanks to my wife Melissa for her editing help, catching incongruities and typos, and her endless patience on this and many other projects.

Any inaccuracies, faults, or errors are purely my own.

TABLE OF CONTENTS

Part III: Statesmen

Part IV: Philosophers and Theologians

INTRODUCTION

Nobody drank as much coffee as 19th-century French novelist Honoré de Balzac. He wrote thousands of words a day by drinking up to 50 cups of bitter coffee, usually on an empty stomach.

Balzac was displeased with the state of literature in his country. He was surrounded by Romantic poets and playwrights who emphasized intense emotion. Alexandre Dumas, Victor Hugo, and Walter Scott fetishized epic poetry and verbose language. Syrupy prose flooded the bookshops of Paris. On the other hand, Balzac preferred real human experiences to abstractions. And he preferred *lots* of them – he wrote about everything and everyone in French society from 1815 onward. Balzac presented a massive panorama of French society, painstakingly reconstructing the French urban working class and provincial life. With a journalist's eye, he recorded details of the lives of thousands from every trade, profession, background, and level of social respectability. Balzac described soldiers, aristocrats, workmen, spies, mistresses, and scoundrels. He described décor, clothing, and possessions. His settings included cities, countryside, ports, schools, churches, and prisons.

"If you knew how I work!" he wrote to a friend in 1832 after finishing another volume of his descriptive analysis. "I am a galley slave to pen and ink, a true dealer in ideas."

His result was *La Comédie humaine*, a multi-volume collection of novels and interconnected stories that depicted French society during the Restoration and July Monarchy of 1815-1848. The total collection was over 140 works, with 95 finished novels and 48 unfinished works. It was the largest literary endeavor undertaken by one person in history. It totaled 24 volumes, published as a definitive edition between 1869 and 1876.

And in order to record everything in his world, Balzac ran his coffee pot non-stop. He drank enough coffee to keep a late-shift fire brigade awake, consuming the aforementioned 50 cups a day, sometimes two cups at a time, on an empty stomach. The caffeine helped Balzac keep up a legendary work habit. He ate a light meal at 6 pm, slept until midnight, then awoke and worked up to 15 hours straight. Once he claimed to have worked 48 hours continuously with only a three-hour rest in the middle.

Balzac's liquid muse had such a grip on his life that he wrote about the complicated relationship in an essay "The Pleasures and Pains of Coffee." He first praises the elixir as setting the blood in motion, chasing away sleep, and giving the capacity to engage a little longer in intellectual exercise. But this was not enough. Balzac then writes of the horrific effects that coffee has on an empty stomach, enough to make an addict of intravenous drugs cringe:

Coffee falls into your stomach, a sack whose velvety interior is lined with tapestries of suckers and papillae. The coffee finds nothing else in the sack, and so it attacks these delicate and voluptuous linings; it acts like a food and demands digestive juices; it wrings and twists the stomach for these juices... it brutalizes these beautiful stomach linings as a wagon master abuses ponies; the plexus becomes inflamed; sparks shoot all the way up to the brain. From that moment on, everything becomes agitated. Ideas quick-march into motion like battalions of a grand army to its legendary fighting ground, and the battle rages... the paper is spread with ink - for the nightly labor begins and ends with torrents of this black water, as a battle opens and concludes with black powder.

Balzac died relatively young, likely due to ailments from his poor sleep patterns and inhuman consumption of the liquid. But his influence on literature cannot be questioned. Despite lacking a patron, he left behind enough writings to fill several library shelves. Whether or not coffee was the secret to his profligacy, his sheer level of output earned him a reputation as a literary giant.

Another ambitious figure comes from a completely different time and place than Balzac, but his level of output is similar. Mimar Sinan, the imperial architect of the Ottoman Empire during the 1500s, constructed or supervised 476 buildings in his lifetime. In comparison, a contemporary Italian master architect might only design a few basilicas. Sinan was the head of the corps of Court Architects. He spent 50 years designing mosques, palaces, tombs, schools, harems, almshouses, madrassahs, caravan palaces, fountains, granaries, aqueducts, and hospitals. His mosques still dominate the skyline of Istanbul's historical district. His buildings represent the high-water mark of classical Ottoman architecture with a geometrical purity and spatial integrity.

Most impressive from Sinan's legacy is the Süleymaniye, the imperial mosque built in honor of the Sultan Süleyman. The sultan commissioned as an enduring structure greater than all the other mosques in the city. Süleyman gave Mimar Sinan near limitless funding for the mosque, which he decreed would have services for city dwellers, including four colleges, a soup kitchen, a hospital, an asylum, a Turkish bath, and even lodgings for travelers. Sinan finished the massive building in only seven years. The domed structure challenges the nearby Haghia Sophia Cathedral in grandeur and dominates the skyline of Istanbul to this day.

Sinan's ability to design hundreds of mosques came from the ability to juggle multiple projects at once. While overseeing the construction of the Süleymaniye Mosque, he took small breaks to design smaller buildings. Local architects took his plans and implemented them, working from rough sketches and filling in the rest of the design plans with their own stylistic choices. He never even saw many of his famous buildings outside of Istanbul even though they bear his name. Whether Sinan was a talented manager of subordinates or guilty of taking credit for the work of others remains open to debate. But nobody debates that his buildings are the greatest surviving architectural heritage from the Ottoman classical age of the 1500s. They cover the domains of the former Ottoman Empire, from Saudi Arabia and Syria to Armenia and Hungary.

Sinan and Balzac's lives had little in common despite their incredible productivity. Their life output bested others by a factor of 10 or even 100. Balzac almost single-handedly defined a genre of French literature. Sinan defined Ottoman architecture and filled the empire with enough buildings to challenge Europe for cultural grandeur. But how did they do it? Beyond drinking gallons of coffee or having an office full of subordinates, how did these two accomplish as much in one year as most professionals achieve in their lives? Did they have tremendous intellectual abilities, or is there another factor that caused them to achieve so much?

This book will explore the lives of the 17 most productive people in history. We will look at their biographies, understand the cultural context into which they were born, and see the methods that they used to achieve such sweeping results. Their exact processes for achievement will be broken down and analyzed on a day-to-day, or even hour-to-hour basis. This will be an easy process to determine with some figures. Benjamin Franklin and Charles Spurgeon left behind autobiographies in which they boasted of their profligacy and even included their daily schedules. Others left behind fewer details, but we know enough from their lives to reverse engineer their work patterns.

First, a note on how this book defines productivity. It is not a measure of total amount of hours per day labored. Many people throughout history worked long hours. Subsistence farmers routinely put in 16-hour days before the Industrial Revolution (although not year-round). Slaves from the Roman era to the Antebellum South were routinely worked to death. Rather, productivity is considered in terms of effectiveness – doing the goal-oriented work that goes about achieving the *right* tasks, not merely doing lots of tasks.

Consider the difference between Dave Tomar and Isaac Asimov. Tomar is the author of the 2012 book "The Shadow Scholar: How I Made A Living Helping College Kids Cheat." He spent a decade as a writer-for-hire for lazy students, producing term papers, essays, and even dissertations at a blinding speed. Tomar wrote up to five pages of academic text an hour, producing hundreds of thousands of words a year.

Isaac Asimov probably wrote no faster. But *what* he wrote is of critical difference. He produced over 500 books over the course of his life in almost every category of the Dewey Decimal System. Many are classics of the science fiction genre. His Foundation Series tops most lists of the greatest works of science fiction in the 20th century. He inspired two generations of Cold War-era youth to take up a study of science.

In the profiles ahead, you will learn from the Issac Asimovs, not the Dave Tomars of the world. This book will consider figures from across history and professional backgrounds. Archimedes was a Greek scientist and mathematician who lived in 3rd-century BC Sicily and observed mathematical phenomena that were not confirmed for another 17 centuries. Emperor Justinian ruled the Byzantine Empire during the 6th century and attempted to resurrect the Western

Roman Empire. Ibn Sina was a medieval mathematician who wrote hundreds of treatises, including a medical compendium used in European universities for the next 400 years. Philipp II of Spain ruled a global empire from his throne in Madrid in the 1500s. Charles Spurgeon was a 19th-century English pastor who pastored a church of more than 10,000 and whose sermons sold 50 million copies. Isaac Newton invented classical physics and was one of the inventors of calculus. Benjamin Franklin wrote, published, politicked, invented, experimented, and humored, sometimes all at the same time. Theodore Roosevelt won the presidency twice, was the first American to earn a belt in judo, hunted, wrote numerous books, and read four hours a day even during the busiest moments of his political life. For good measure he also won a Nobel Peace Prize and was the first sitting president to leave the United States during his term in order to visit the Panama Canal works.

Some of these figures were productive because of their incredible intelligence. Medieval theologian Thomas Aquinas claimed that he remembered everything he read, so that his mind was like a huge library. He could reportedly dictate to five scribes at the same time on five different books. Napoleon Bonaparte rose through the ranks of the French army largely because of his remarkable memory. In an 1805 campaign, a subordinate could not locate his division. Napoleon told the officer his unit's present location, where he would be stationed for the next three nights, his unit's strength, and the subordinate's military record. This, despite the fact that the subordinate was one of 200,000 soldiers, and their units were constantly on the move.

Others achieved their productivity by workaholism. Thomas Edison rarely slept except at his workbench, catching a 2-hour nap after 20 or more hours of continuous experiments. Charles Spurgeon frequently worked 18 hours a day. He wrote over 500 letters a week, and preached 10 times a week. He never took a day of rest except when his health became so poor that his body forced him into a bed-ridden state. Once healed he immediately resumed his frenetic schedule. Elon Musk is CEO of both a rocket and electric car company. He manages them by working 100+ hours a week. Time spent with his five children is also spent on his smart phone answering emails.

But workaholism is not a prerequisite for productivity. Some produced spectacularly through highly structured daily schedules. Benjamin Franklin woke at 5 am every day to breakfast and plan the day, then began working at 8 am, worked more from 2 to 5 pm, then stopped at 6 pm. Thomas Aquinas lived in a friary and had the exact moments of his life dictated by the rules of his holy order. Provided he was not traveling, Thomas knew exactly what he was doing at each hour. Isaac Asimov began writing at 6 am and produced at least 5,000 words a day regardless of their quality. He learned this habit as a child when working at his Russian father's candy store, which opened each day at from 6 am in order to cater to the hours of its urban clientele.

They also accomplished much by delegating tasks to those around them. Julius Caesar wrote a historical account of the Gallic Wars while leading military expeditions by dictating letters to scribes on horseback. Pliny the Elder says that he used to dictate four letters at once, and even up to seven during particularly busy periods. By these means he was able to write his detailed formal reports to the Senate and his *Commentaries of the Gallic Wars*, published in a seven-volume set. Thomas Edison had many assistants involved with his projects, enabling him to file over a thousand patents and accumulate 5 million pages of records. His organizational abilities allowed him to institutionalize his creative designs, pass them on to assistants, and multiply his effectiveness.

Most of all, the highly productive figures of history were able to do so much because they are driven by a larger goal. Each day, week, month, and year was subordinated to a greater purpose. This life vision helped them push through difficult periods. Religious figures such as Aquinas and Ibn Sina believed their work to serve the cause of God and bring glory to him. Justinian believed his reign could resurrect the Roman Empire. Elon Musk pours his life into his rocket design company SpaceX in order to colonize Mars and make humanity a multi-planet species. They understood that productivity is not an accident but rather a result of a focused effort.

While few of us will ever be able to achieve the level of output of the figures in this book, there are many lessons for us to apply. These stories can help us focus on efforts that actually make a difference versus those that are mere busy work. They can teach us ways to become *entrepreneurs* in the technical sense of the word – to shift assets from unproductive areas to productive areas. Perhaps with their examples in mind, we can create enough time to focus on the tasks in life that are truly meaningful. Franz Kafka said, "Productivity is being able to do things that you were never able to do before." The productive geniuses you are about to meet can show us the way.

Part I

Scientists and Inventors

CHAPTER ONE

ARCHIMEDES (287-212 BC)

The Norwegian town of Rjukan sits in darkness six months of the year. Located in a valley, its 3,000 residents spend half their lives in perpetual shadow. But the town is doing something to capture the sun's rays and shine light into its square. To brighten their gloomy winters, Rjukan's residents installed three 550-square-foot mirrors to reflect sunlight on the town below.

"The square will become a sunny meeting place in a town otherwise in a shadow," Rjkhan's official website states. Mirrors reflecting an ellipse of bright light are each guided by a computer that follows the sun's path. For the first time ever, the winter sun now shines on the town.

"It's the sun!" said retired secretary Ingrid Sparbo, lifting her face to the light and closing her eyes against the glare. Sparbo has lived all her life in Rjukan. She said to the Guardian that people "do sort of get used to the shade. You end up not thinking about it, really. But this ... this is so warming. Not just physically, but mentally. It's mentally warming."

The mirrors can also be physically warming. Or physically scalding. They can even produce enough light to create a solar-powered death ray. And this idea for weaponized solar combat is not new. It traces back to a third-century BC legend of Archimedes using such mirrors to set Roman battle ships on fire.

According to the tale, Archimedes, already a famed inventor, destroyed the naval might of the Romans with his ingenuity. In 212 BC Rome had laid siege to Syracuse. Then the Sicilian mathematical genius rolled out a giant round mirror, flanked by smaller mirrors. The reflective surfaces concentrated the sun's rays on the wooden ships, building up to a primitive laser. The solar ray gained enough concentration to kindle a flame and burn the entire Roman fleet.

Researchers have wondered for centuries whether the story was a myth. So in 2006, an MIT professor and his students attempted to find out. They started with materials found in a Roman vessel, mostly wood and oakum soaked in pitch. A parabolic mirror was fashioned to recreate the ancient solar laser. But the team failed to produce the ready combustion they hoped for. They produced nothing more than smoke at a distance of 150 feet from the boats and only achieved ignition at 75 feet. While other researchers have had better success with reenactments of Archimedes's mirrors, nobody has achieved the same success as he is recorded to have created. The ancient death ray is likely a myth. But that the myth is so widely believed is more of a testimony to the legend of Archimedes' genius than the technological plausibility of Roman-era solar weaponry.

His reputation is well deserved. Archimedes' practical applications of physics run from water displacement to catapults. Many of his inventions are still in use today: the compound pulley is still the basic mechanical feature of an elevator. He invented a screw that moved water uphill and catapults that defended Syracuse from Roman invaders. Cicero reports that he saw a planetarium in Syracuse that was built by Archimedes. It displayed the motions of the sun, the moon, and the five known planets. Its accuracy was so great that it could show the phases of the moon and predicted eclipses of the sun and the moon.

His discoveries in mathematics reach the upper limits of discoverability without the aid of algebra and analytical geometry which weren't systematized until 17 centuries after his death. He determined the area of a circle, the surface area of a sphere, the area under a parabola, the value of pi, and rudimentary calculus. "Archimedes was the greatest mathematician in the ancient world," said William Noel, a curator of ancient manuscripts at the Walters Art Museum in Baltimore. "He was the first scientist to apply abstract mathematical principles to the world around him."

He continues to surprise researchers. A lost writing of Archimedes resurfaced in 1998, which scientists deciphered by using X-rays, ultraviolet light, and other enhanced imaging techniques. The document includes treatises such as *"The Method of Mechanical Theorems," "On Floating Bodies,"* and *"Stomachion,"* which identifies the number of different ways to solve a children's puzzle. In *"Mechanical Theorems,"* he derived an object's geometrical and physical properties by observing the way it balances. The method describes infinity, which historians of science long held was too problematic for Greek mathematicians to comprehend until the time of Isaac Newton and Gottfried Wilhelm von Leibniz.

Best of all, Archimedes had a strange personality to match his genius. The Smithsonian magazine notes that he may be best known for leaping up from his bath and running naked through the city, shouting *Eureka!* which means, "I have found it!" (And what had he found? He had just discovered he could determine the proportion of gold and silver in Heiron's wreath by measuring the volume of water it displaced.)

How did Archimedes accomplish so much while avoiding arrest for public indecency when he lived in a Mediterranean backwater with little access to technological tools or written works to carry on his studies? With no fellow scientists or reference manuals to help him, he was forced to make his discoveries *sui generis*. It would be as if one inventor accomplished the technical feats of Edison and the theoretical feats of Newton while living among tribesmen in New Guinea.

Because of the scarcity of surviving sources from the ancient world, we do not know as much about Archimedes' daily habits as more recent figures like Theodore Roosevelt or Benjamin Franklin. However, many principles of productivity can be derived from Archimedes' life. First, he had exceptional focus. He entered a trance-like phase during his research, becoming unaware of anything else around him. Archimedes often did not sleep while focusing on a mathematical or mechanical difficulty. He forgot to eat. His servants had to drag him to his bath in order to bathe him and anoint him with oil. Even this did not stop him. While bathing he continued to draw geometrical figures on any surface possible, whether the nearby dirt or even his own oil-slicked body. His mental ability to dim any non-worked related issues perhaps explains his lack of shame while streaking through Syracuse. It also explains the manner of his death, which we will explore later in this chapter.

But he many have been pushed to be a productive genius out of necessity. His role as a crafty inventor came about due to Syracuse's needs of advanced military science. The Mediterranean island of Sicily was sandwiched between Carthage and Rome, an unfortunate location during the Punic Wars. Islands between these empires were subject to conquest, settlement, quartering of enemy troops, and nasty sieges. Syracuse needed weaponry to project power that exceeded the strength of its small military.

Archimedes was up to the task. He assembled some of the most terrifying weapons of the ancient world. According to some ancient historians, his solar-powered laser was one of many inventions to intimidate Rome's superior army and Carthage's navy. Another such weapon was his long range catapult, built during the two-year Roman Siege of Syracuse in 214-212 BC.

The attack on Syracuse came during the Second Punic War. Rome feared that Syracuse, located on the east coast of Sicily, would forge an alliance with Carthage, so Rome decided to take the city first.

Archimedes had other plans. He crafted an assault strategy that would strike the approaching Roman naval fleet during the stages of its approach. Short-range weaponry would then pummel any ships or soldiers that managed to reach the city walls.

The elderly inventor first devised long-range artillery to attack the ships. He developed advanced catapults, capable of delivering a heavier payload. Some rocks weighed as much as 500 pounds. They were fired at the base of ships and siege engines, causing massive damage while the Roman fleet was still at a great distance from Syracuse. Historian Polybius notes that Archimedes scored so many hits with his catapults and stone-throwers that he slowed their approach to a crawl.

The next step was to defend the city walls. Syracuse was renowned for its great fortifications so the Romans prepared to counter this obstacle. They brought their own inventive devices to aid the assault. Among these were the *sambuca*, a floating siege tower with grappling hooks, and ship-mounted scaling ladders that were lowered with pulleys onto the city walls.

Archimedes' response was even more terrifying. His answer to the *sambuca* was the Claw of Archimedes – an enormous crane equipped with a grappling hook able to lift attacking ships out of the water. To a horrified sailor, it appeared as though the arm of a god had emerged from behind the city walls. The Claw then crushed the ship in its "palm," smashed it against the rocks, or suddenly dropped it, causing it to capsize.

Plutarch describes the effects of the Claw as follows.

....Others were seized at the prow by iron claws, or beaks like the beaks of cranes, drawn straight up into the air, and then plunged stern foremost into the depths, or were turned round and round by means of enginery within the city, and dashed upon the steep cliffs that jutted out beneath the wall of the city, with great destruction of the fighting men on board, who perished in the wrecks. Frequently, too, a ship would be lifted out of the water into mid-air, whirled hither and thither as it hung there, a dreadful spectacle, until its crew had been thrown out and hurled in all directions, when it would fall empty upon the walls, or slip away from the clutch that had held it.

Ships that managed to avoid the first barrage of catapult fire or the Claw of Archimedes had to contend with the next level of defense. It was a layered array of projectile weapons known as "the scorpions." In order to prevent the Romans from climbing up the city walls at night, Archimedes ordered that a series of holes be drilled across the walls. Small-scale catapults could be brought bear on objects close at hand without being seen. The loopholes within the walls were only the breadth of a palm width. Archers behind the walls also discharged large crossbows to fire iron darts at the Romans. There was, Plutarch writes, "a great slaughter among [the Romans]; many of their ships, too, were dashed together, and they could not retaliate in any way upon their foes."

The advanced weapons diminished the morale of the Roman invaders. General Marcellus, the Roman commander, said to his engineers, "Let us stop fighting against this geometrical Briareus, who uses our ships like cups to ladle water from the sea... and with the many missiles which he shoots against us all at once, outdoes the hundred-handed monsters of mythology."

Plutarch writes that Archimedes' role in the assault was so critical that he alone provided for the defense of the city. He was the one soul moving and managing everything; all other weapons lay idle.

Plutarch writes that whenever the Romans saw a bit of rope or a stick of timber projecting a little over the wall, they shouted "There it is! Archimedes is training some engine upon us!" The Romans soon abandoned their assault and settled down for a long siege.

By far Archimedes' most devastating weapon was the death ray. As described earlier, ancient historians write that the engineer arranged a set of many small, flat mirrors. According to Byzantine author Tzetzes he constructed a kind of hexagonal mirror and at an interval proportionate to the size of the mirror. Archimedes set similar small mirrors with four edges, moving by links and by a kind of hinge. He made the glass the center of the sun's rays, concentrating the energy into a beam and reducing ships to ashes.

The weapon makes for a thrilling account and makes Archimedes sound like a James Bond villain. But is it fact or fiction? There are doubts from historians and scientists. Historians note it is not recorded in the most ancient accounts of Archimedes' life. Livy, Polybius, and Plutarch gave detailed descriptions of the Siege of Syracuse but make no mention of the heat ray. Lucian is the first to mention the weapon, but he wrote four centuries after the siege and was known as a satirist. Anthemius of Tralles first mentioned the use of mirrors only in the sixth century, and Tzetzes' account comes from the twelfth century.

Modern scientists are more skeptical. Researchers in the 20th century have tested whether such an ancient weapon was possible. The results were mixed. One MIT team tried to ignite a mock wooden ship in 2005 but could only produce smoke. In 1973 Greek scientist Ioannis Sakkas performed an experiment in Skaramagas naval base near Athens using 7o copper-coated mirrors, the type that would have existed in Archimedes' day. He redirected sunlight toward a mock plywood ship 200 feet away. The model burst into flames after a few seconds. But Roman ships were larger and made of more durable cedar, suggesting they would have not ignited.

However, whether or not the ray existed, many other treasures continue to surface from Archimedes' life. A 9th-century copy of a previously-unknown mathematical text was recently rediscovered. Known as the *Archimedes Palimpsest*, the original copy was washed by a 13th century monk to make a Christian liturgical text, a common practice since parchment was so rare and expensive at that time. Scientists recovered the text in the 1990s and have been able to restore the original writing underneath through digital processing. They found a manuscript called "On the Sphere and the Cylinder." In it he gives a method for determining the surface area of a sphere by using a technique similar to the Riemann summation, named after the 19th century mathematician Bernhard Riemann.

Another interesting treatise found in Archimedes' lost writing is the "Stomachion." The Smithsonian notes it is arguably the first treatise on combinatorics, a branch of mathematics focused on the organization of elements within sets. Archimedes describes a puzzle in which a square is cut into 14 irregular pieces. He writes on the number of ways the pieces can be arranged back into a square – the puzzle's answer is 17,152. "What we've been finding with the *Archimedes Palimpsest* is that this book never ceases to give up its secrets," says Noel. "It's like working with a great mind; you've made to think of things in new ways—from the nuts and bolts of medieval history to the roots of calculus and physics."

Archimedes continually thought of things in new ways through his single-minded focus on his research. We do not know whether Archimedes studied mathematics for pure intellectual curiosity or due to a patriotic desire to develop technology that would defend the underdog Syracuse from the perpetually hostile Romans. Whatever his reasons, Archimedes remained committed to learning up to the point of his death. According to Valerius Maximus, he was working on a mathematical problem deep into the siege of Syracuse when a Roman soldier burst into his study. He was drawing figures in the dirt, immersed in geometry. Archimedes protected the dust circles with his hands, yelling, "I beg you, don't disturb this!" The soldier responded by sticking him through with his sword. Valerius Maximus adds a dramatic final statement to these last seconds: "...and with his blood he confused the lines of his art. So it fell out that he was first granted his life and then stripped of it by reason of the same pursuit."

The Roman general Marcellus was grieved at news that Archimedes was executed against his orders. Roman historians write that he ordered the execution of the soldier in retaliation and made sure that the Greek scientist was buried with full honors. Marcellus also honored Archimedes's wish that his tombstone bear the image of a sphere within a cylinder. The image represented his discovery of the ratio that the volume of a sphere is two-thirds the volume of the smaller cylinder that encloses it, and that likewise the surface of the sphere is also two-thirds the surface area of the cylinder.

Even after death, Archimedes made sure others were reminded of his work, maintaining his focus beyond his life.

CHAPTER TWO

ISAAC NEWTON (1642-1726)

Isaac Newton's genius dominates the first two years of any university curriculum in the hard sciences. He was one of the inventors of calculus. He revolutionized optics by determining that white light was not a single color but all the colors of light combined. He invented classical physics in his tract *Philosophiae Naturalis Principia Mathematica* while at home when Cambridge University was forced to shut down. He wrote formulas of the mathematical constant of gravity while observing an apple falling from a tree. From this sprung laws of planetary motion and all movement in the observable universe.

Newton was so productive as a mathematician that he made discoveries that scientists did not fully appreciate until 300 years later. With all this success he did what any self-respecting natural philosopher would do – spend the latter part of his life locked away in his house learning alchemy and locking down the date of the apocalypse. But despite Newton's strange behavior in the final stages of his life, he accomplished more than any modern theorist, save Einstein.

This was all the more remarkable considering his upbringing.

Newton was born on Christmas Day, 1642, at Woolsthorpe, a village in Lincolnshire, England. His father died two months before he was born. He studied a basic education at a local school. Newton was sent to King's School in Grantham at the age of 12. He lived in the home of a pharmacist named Clark who had a chemical collection from which Newton pilfered to perform experiments. Newton's mother returned to Woolsthorpe and pulled him out of school to help run the family farm, but he was too interested in books to be an effective farmer. At the age of 19 he entered Trinity College, Cambridge, where he learned of the scientific revolution launched by Copernicus, Kepler, and Galileo. He studied natural philosophy and theology, then returned home after his 1665 graduation to escape the plague sweeping the country.

Newton's manuscript collection shows a diverse array of intellectual interests as a youth. His *Pierpont Morgan Notebook*, which begin in 1659, is filled with recipes, formulas, and instructions for performing simple conjuring tricks. In one passage he explains how to turn water into wine with instructions to take "as much lockwood as you can hold in your mouth without discovery, tye it up in a cloth & put it in your mouth, then sup up some wather & champe the lockwood 3 or 4 times & doe it out into a glass."

His varied interests caused him to become bored with Cambridge's rigid curriculum. He disregarded the subjects required in his first year of studies – primarily the ethics and natural philosophy of Aristotle – causing his early instructors to consider him a poor student. Not until mathematics professor Isaac Barrow recognized his genius did Newton's scholarly career begin in earnest. Newton's notebook evidences his intellectual preferences. It begins with a series of notes on Aristotle then abruptly changes and discusses Descartes's latest theories on science and mathematics.

In 1665 the plague broke out in London. The university was closed for 18 months, and Newton returned to his family estate. While in Lincolnshire, he entered the first of his exceptionally productive periods, still in his mid-20s. Newton generalized the results of the binomial theorem in mathematics. He established the early foundations of calculus. He developed his ideas of light, color, and its effects on optics. Newton's observation of a falling apple planted the seed in his mind of a theory of universal gravity. When he returned to Cambridge, Newton published his book *Opticks*. He theorized that light was made of particles and white light composed of many colors, challenging the prevailing theory of the day that light consisted of waves.

In 1687 he published his work on planetary motion and the movement of heavenly bodies. Newton formulated his laws of motion and used calculus to derive Kepler's law of planetary motion from an inverse-square force law of gravity. These same principles were used to explain the shape of the earth, the motion of comets, and even the irregular orbit of the moon. For the next 250 years, his theories of planetary motion were the guiding light of astronomy. They were only usurped when quantum mechanics and relativity offered explanations for the behavior of objects traveling very fast in relation to each other.

But his research still speaks to any practical physicist. In 2014 the European Space Agency deployed the Philae lander on a comet as part of its Rosetta mission. Newton's theory of gravity played a critical role in the probe's soft landing. His equations on orbital mechanics were used by the processors of the probe to determine its movement in relation to comet 67P/Churyumov–Gerasimenko. "It's all down to Isaac Newton now," said European Space Agency senior science advisor Mark McCaughrean before Philae touched down. "It's down to the laws of physics."

Newton made numerous scientific breakthroughs for a few reasons. He allowed rational inquiry to take him in whatever direction that it led. His rival Gottfried Leibniz rejected his theory of gravity because it did not explain how gravity worked across empty space. Newton replied that the question of "why" was irrelevant to the question of "how." He famously replied that he did not know what gravity was, he was only formulating a mathematical description of its behavior. The "why" did not come until the early 20th century with Einstein's discovery of spacetime curvature.

This open-minded approach to research also led him down paths of inquiry that modern thinkers would consider ridiculous, such as alchemy. But in order to appreciate the full scope of Newton's productivity, it is useful to take a detour and explore his research into his alchemical studies. Since his other scientific theories also received intense criticism that bordered on the malicious, Newton was not afraid to approach fields that were under attack.

Alchemy had a poor reputation in 17th century England. Charlatans claimed knowledge of it, promising nobility and royal families to turn their lead into gold. Newton's approach to alchemy was far more encompassing. To him, it was a field of study that could explain the mysteries of the physical and spiritual universe. Alchemy at its core is the study of transmutation. Most researchers were only interested in the transmutation of cheap metals into gold, but Newton was interested in alchemy's spiritual dimensions; of transmuting a lowly soul into a mature soul.

He wrote about quintessence, the formless base of all matter that God used in creation. Alchemy was the study of breaking matter down to get to this *prima materia* and building it back up to whatever the researcher wanted. By understanding the working mechanics of matter, Newton believed he could find the nexus between the material and immaterial worlds. He wrote 5,000 pages on alchemy, or about 1 million words, representing 10 percent of his surviving writings. John Maynard Keynes, who collected and studied much of Newton's writings, claimed that "Sir Isaac believed the universe is a cryptogram set by the Almighty."

By the time of his death in 1727, Newton left behind a stack of papers containing an estimated 10 million words, enough to fill 150 full-length books. Many of Newton's writings on alchemy were found in this stack, along with views of religion that were deeply unorthodox. He wrote a forensic analysis of the Bible in an effort to decode divine prophecies. He analyzed the exact dimensions of Solomon's Temple, looking for clues on the exact date of Judgment Day, settling on the year 2060. He rejected the doctrine of the Trinity, believing the union of the Father, Son, and Holy Spirit was not repeated in nature as it would have been if there were a Triune God. His heir John Conduitt, the husband of his half-niece Catherine Barton, hid this work. Conduitt feared the respected scientist would be thought of as a crackpot and heretic.

When Newton's papers came to Cambridge in the 1800s, modern researchers were horrified. Here was Newton, one of the fathers of the Enlightenment and the shining star of rationality. And he was scribbling thousands of pages on occult science that nobody in polite society could mention, let alone claim as their most important research. When John Couch Adams, the co-discovered of Neptune, and George Stokes were confronted with these papers they were dismayed. Sarah Dry recounts their reaction in her book *The Newton Papers: The Strange and True Odyssey of Isaac Newton's Manuscripts*. The two researchers noted that Newton would sometimes produce six or seven copies of the same tract on alchemy. They were disappointed at seeing their intellectual father copying the same thing over and over again, like discovering a beloved celebrity secretly believing the moon landing was faked.

Adams and Stokes dealt with the contradiction by dismissed his strange habits as mere practice in penmanship, nothing more. "His power of writing a beautiful hand was evidently a snare to him."

But the same open-mindedness that cause Newton to empty ink wells writing tracts on alchemy also allowed him to discover mathematical theories that took centuries to fully appreciate. In

Book I of the *Principia* there is a mathematical result about the algebraic non-integrability of smooth ovals. This result was not appreciated until it was rediscovered 300 years later. Newton made a topological argument long before such a form of topology was invented. This was the first impossibility proof since the ancient Greeks.

Newton found other ways to help the world centuries after his death. In the 1920s financial analyst Roger Babson based his market research on Newtonian principles, using the idea that for every action there is an equal and opposite reaction. He became rich predicting the crash of 1929. Much like Newton, he also took these ideas into strange directions. Babson thought of gravity as an evil scourge. He blamed gravity as the culprit that caused his relatives to drown. To honor their memory, he established the Gravity Research Foundation, which went on to do research in anti-gravity technology.

Beyond his open-mindedness, Newton had more practical habits that made him such an effective scientist. He organized his research through meticulous record keeping. He kept track of his theoretical analyses by producing up to 100 pages of notes a day. *The Newton Project*, a digital humanities research project, has catalogued 4.2 million published and unpublished words by Newton, many of which are made available as downloadable interactive transcriptions. They are a densely written collection of writings in physics, mathematics, and theology.

Newton's habit of note-taking began at a young age. He shared Benjamin Franklin's belief that recording one's poor behavior could lead to self-improvement. Among his early entries are a list of 49 sins that he admittedly committed before "Whitsunday." His list reveals a deeply pious man who struggled to reconcile his irascible nature with a commitment to obedience before God. His confessions included:

BEFORE WHITSUNDAY 1662

1. Using the word (God) openly
2. Eating an apple at Thy house
3. Making a feather while on Thy day
4. Denying that I made it
5. Making a mousetrap on Thy day
6. Contriving of the chimes on Thy day
7. Squirting water on Thy day
8. Making pies on Sunday night
9. Swimming in a kimnel on Thy day
10. Putting a pin in Iohn Keys hat on Thy day to pick him
11. Carelessly hearing and committing many sermons
12. Refusing to go to the close at my mothers command
13. Threatning my father and mother Smith to burne them and the house over them
14. Wishing death and hoping it to some
15. Striking many
16. Having uncleane thoughts words and actions and dreamese
17. Stealing cherry cobs from Eduard Storer
18. Denying that I did so
19. Denying a crossbow to my mother and grandmother though I knew of it
20. Setting my heart on money learning pleasure more than Thee
21. A relapse
22. A relapse
23. A breaking again of my covenant renued in the Lords Supper
24. Punching my sister
25. Robbing my mothers box of plums and sugar
26. Calling Dorothy Rose a jade
27. Glutiny in my sickness
28. Peevishness with my mother

29. With my sister
30. Falling out with the servants
31. Divers commissions of alle my duties
32. Idle discourse on Thy day and at other times
33. Not turning nearer to Thee for my affections
34. Not living according to my belief
35. Not loving Thee for Thy self
36. Not loving Thee for Thy goodness to us
37. Not desiring Thy ordinances
38. Not long [longing] for Thee in [illegible]
39. Fearing man above Thee
40. Using unlawful means to bring us out of distresses
41. Caring for worldly things more than God
42. Not craving a blessing from God on our honest endeavors
43. Missing chapel
44. Beating Arthur Storer
45. Peevishness at Master Clarks for a piece of bread and butter
46. Striving to cheat with a brass halfe crowne
47. Twisting a cord on Sunday morning
48. Reading the history of the Christian champions on Sunday

Many of these "sins" appear so trifling as to border on the ridiculous. But whatever our judgment on the pernicious nature of "idle discourse," his record keeping had surprising results. Newton's recording of his own sins apparently had a positive effect on his character. He repeated the process after Whitsunday and recorded only nine sins. While he never achieved moral perfection in life, he used the same concept of note-taking-as-moral-improvement as Benjamin Franklin did a century later. Recording his own behavior made him aware of his actions, resulting in less self-diagnosed bad behavior.

Beyond self-auditing, Newton managed strong feats of productivity due to his reclusive character. He was deeply introverted and protective of his privacy. He remained insecure throughout his life due to a troubled childhood and early death of his father. Newton was given to fits of violent temper and depression, deeply distrusting those around him. He worked to destroy the reputation of Gottfried Leibniz, who independently discovered the principles of calculus, believing him to have stolen them. Some of this paranoia was justifiable. Researchers of the time had to contend with intense criticism from their competitors, much of it malicious. But his prickly temperament and misanthropy only intensified his paranoia.

Newton had a nervous breakdown in 1693. After five nights of no sleep, he lost connection with reality and believed his friends Locke and Pepys were attempting to assassinate him. His manic episode was so bad that Locke later confessed to Newton that during his fits, "when one told me you were sickly... I answered t'were better if you were dead."

Newton's academic rivalries extended to his work on optics. He was enraged that the accuracy of his observations were questioned by two French Jesuits, Francis Linus and Ignace Pardies. Both misunderstood his research and were eventually refuted. Then Christiaan Huygens and Royal Society Curator of Experiments Robert Hooke questioned his data, claiming he had not performed enough experiments. Newton was so troubled by this criticism that he threatened to completely withdrawal from public discussion of natural philosophy. He carried a bitter public feud with Hooke, which intensified when the latter accused Newton of plagiarizing his idea of a gravitational inverse square relationship, relating the force between bodies to their distance from each other. The feud continued until Hooke's death in 1703.

Due to Newton's protective secretiveness he left behind no private diaries and little private correspondence. We cannot look deep into his inner life and know his work habits because he tells us so little. Historians had to be satisfied with his published works. But his published works are so densely written that they left kept historians of science busy for decades. Astrophysicist and Nobel laureate Subrahmanyan Chandrasekhar (1910-1995) spent the last five years of his life reading the *Principia* and decoding it for modern physicists. He could only decode the most important sections. The reason that the *Principia* is so difficult for modern audiences is its writing style. Newton presented his proofs in a geometrical form used by the ancient Greeks instead of the algebraic form used by scientists today. William Whewell (1794-1866) commented on this aspect of Newton's work.

> Nobody since Newton has been able to use geometrical methods to the same extent for the like purposes; and as we read the *Principia* we feel as when we are in an ancient armoury where the weapons are of gigantic size; and as we look at them we marvel what manner of man he was who could use as a weapon what we can scarcely lift as a burden.

Despite his troubled personal life, Newton's imitable legacy is his genius in many fields, which was highlighted by his great productivity. Because of this he has even inspired a number of 21st-century management experts. Consultants James Clear and Cody Wheeler applied Newton's three laws of physics to increasing personal efficiency.

For instance, they applied Newton's principle that objects in motion tend to stay in motion unless acted upon by an outside force. The application is to focus on nothing else but getting started. Once a task begins, its doer will likely carry it on to completion. Clear has further distilled this physics-as-productivity principle into the 2-Minute Rule: To overcome procrastination, find a way to start your task in less than two minutes. Once you start it is simpler to keep moving. Momentum will do the work.

The second principle, force equals mass times acceleration, translates to applying effort in areas of life that are most effective. Where a person places force is equally as important as how hard he or she works. Hard work itself is not sufficient; work must be applied in effective ways.

The third law of motion – where one body exerts a force on a second body, the second body exerts equal force on the first body – means that one should eliminate opposing forces such as inefficient tasks.

Few 17th-century physicists can say they inspire 21st century efficiency experts today. But little about Newton was ordinary.

CHAPTER THREE

BENJAMIN FRANKLIN (1706-1790)

Benjamin Franklin was nothing if not diversified in his talents. The Founding Father was a printer, scientist, inventor, diplomat, postmaster general, educator, philosopher, entrepreneur, library curator, and America's first researcher to win an international scientific reputation for his studies in electrical theory. He even made contributions to knowledge of the Gulf Stream.

His inventions shaped American colonial life. Perhaps his most famous invention was the Franklin stove. Most fireplaces at the time concentrated heat, leaving the area around the fireplace scorching hot and the rest of the house frigid. Franklin's stove, invented in 1742, remained in the fireplace but its grate protruded into the room, diffusing heat throughout the house. Franklin refused to patent the stove, believing it should be used freely throughout the colonies. Later versions became fixtures in houses of that era and remained popular throughout the 1800s.

More interestingly, Benjamin Franklin was perhaps the most moral man who ever published an article on how to select a mistress.

The proper title of his 1745 article was "Advice to a Young Man on the Choice of a Mistress." After a preamble in which he commits to a half-hearted attempt at convincing his young interlocutor not to take a mistress, he then advises him to take a middle-aged paramour over a younger one. Among the eight reasons he offers, two stand out. First, there is no hazard of children, "which irregularly prduc'd may be attended with much Inconvenience." Second, and more to the point, because the middle-aged are so grateful for the attention.

The advice appears to be based on Franklin's direct experience, and we must note that he was equally thorough in other pursuits. This allowed him to attain enormous wealth at a young age. His scientific and literary fame spread to the European continent, where he was known for particularly for his humorous writings and also for his published experiments on electricity. When war broke out against England, Franklin assisted in the drafting of the Declaration of Independence and the Constitution. He parlayed this fame into an ambassadorial career to France during the American Revolution.

Franklin was born in 1706 as the fifteenth son of Josiah, a soap and candlemaker. He began to assist his father in his shop at age 10, performing duties such as cutting candle wicks and filling molds. He only attended school for two years but devoured books on his own and taught himself to invent simple devices. At age 12 he apprenticed in his half-brother James's print shop. He continued to study grammar, navigation, and arithmetic and practiced drafting political essays when not busy with other duties. To improve his own writing he studied *Spectator* essays by Joseph Addison and Richard Steele, copied a particularly good article, and rewrote it in his own style, then compared his essay with the original to understand the mechanics of good composition.

During this time he began to write letters to *The New England Courant*, a paper James produced, considered the first truly independent newspaper in the colonies. He wrote under the pen name "Mrs. Silence Dogood," a middle-aged widow who satirized Boston society. Franklin soon developed a large following. Readers were shocked when the precocious adolescent's identity was revealed. He then experienced a falling out with James by leaving his apprenticeship without his brother's permission, thus beginning a life of travel.

Franklin spent the next several years bouncing between Boston, Philadelphia, and London and supporting himself as a printer and sales clerk. Over the next two decades he planted the seeds of a publishing empire. He was made the official printer for Pennsylvania and later Maryland. Franklin built the first newspaper chain by constructing a network of print shops from New England to the Carolinas. The most popular of his publications was *Poor Richard's Almanac*, a farmer's guide that included weather forecasts and witticisms. He sold 10,000 copies a year, a best-seller second only to the Bible at the time. Here was first published Franklin's famous maxim "Early to bed, early to rise makes a man healthy, wealthy, and wise."

Printing to him had a public-service function in addition to being a profitable venture. He saw the printing press as a means to build up the colonies' moral virtue. Historian Ralph Frasca argues that Franklin understood morality in terms of action, and saw work such as a printing as a service to God. Despite his moral failings – and expert knowledge on dalliances with middle-aged women – he believed himself uniquely knowledgeable about instructing Americans in morality.

For this reason he talks much about personal productivity much in his writings. In his autobiography, Franklin described in detail his daily schedule, perhaps in order to inspire his readers. He writes that in order to maximize productivity, one must give marching orders to each part of the day. Franklin's own daily schedule was divided down to smaller chunks. No part of the day was left without a specified task. It all began with a simple question each morning: What good shall I do this day? From then on he answers that question with the particulars of each moment.

Here is his daily schedule that he printed in his autobiography.

5-7 am: Rise, wash, and address *Powerful Goodness*; contrive day's business and take the resolution of the day; prosecute the present study; and breakfast

8-11 am: Work

12-1 pm: Read or overlook my accounts, and dine

2-5 pm: Work

6-9 pm: Put things in their places, supper, music, or diversion, or conversation; examination of the day

10 pm - 5 am: Sleep. Before then, answer the question 'What good have I done today?'

The effectiveness of such a schedule allowed Franklin to achieve mastery in a variety of fields. In 1751 he published his "Experiments and Observations with Electricity," then conducting his kite experiment the following year, proving that thunder and lightening were electrical phenomena. He put up lightening rods around the same time, which protected his buildings from lightening strikes and fires. Philip Dray writes in *Stealing God's Thunder: Benjamin Franklin's Lightening Rod and the Invention of America* that this invention had widespread significance on the colonies: "The lightning rod was one of the Enlightenment's greatest inventions not only for the lives and property it saved, but for its potent symbolism. By subduing nature's most arrogant power, it raised a defining question of the late eighteenth century: If reason can vanquish thunderbolts, can it also influence morality, social organization, and human behavior?"

Franklin believed that reason could lead to not just a perfect daily schedule, but a perfectly virtuous life. Along with his daily plan, he put together a multi-week program of moral improvement that would eventually rid him of bad habits. He believed that an effective life was the result of day-to-day micro-planning along with year-to-year macro-planning focused on improvement of moral character and becoming a completely virtuous person. He resolved that such an extensive undertaking could only be accomplished by breaking poor habits, replacing them with good habits. He thought that becoming morally excellent would lead to a productive life.

While Franklin was not devout in the traditional sense, he was a theist who thought that God was the foundation of wisdom, and maintaining a moral life was the best means to reach a perfect life.

To do so he created the following method of conduct. First, in his readings he identified virtues that were common across Western Civilization. Writers across history and cultures came back to these virtues. For example, one such virtue was temperance. Although the idea found different expression in different settings (temperance sometimes meant complete abstinence from alcohol; other times it meant the moderation of any mental or physical passion) it was universally agreed to be a worthy goal. Then Franklin created his own system of virtue, giving them 13 names and attaching to each of them a short precept that fully expressed the extent he gave to its meaning.

This is his list of virtues.

1. Temperance. Eat not to dullness; drink not to elevation.

2. Silence. Speak not but what may benefit others or yourself; avoid trifling conversation.

3. Order. Let all your things have their places; let each part of your business have its time.

4. Resolution. Resolve to perform what you ought; perform without fail what you resolve.

5. Frugality. Make no expense but to do good to others or yourself; i.e., waste nothing.

6. Industry. Lose no time; be always employ'd in something useful; cut off all unnecessary actions.

7. Sincerity. Use no hurtful deceit; think innocently and justly, and, if you speak, speak accordingly.

8. Justice. Wrong none by doing injuries, or omitting the benefits that are your duty.

9. Moderation. Avoid extremes; forbear resenting injuries so much as you think they deserve.

10. Cleanliness. Tolerate no uncleanliness in body, clothes, or habitation.

11. Tranquility. Be not disturbed at trifles, or at accidents common or unavoidable.

12. Chastity. Rarely use venery but for health or offspring, never to dullness, weakness, or the injury of your own or another's peace or reputation.

13. Humility. Imitate Jesus and Socrates.

Franklin was practical enough to know that tackling all 13 virtues at the same time would lead to discouragement and then failure. He took them on one at a time, only moving on when a virtue was mastered. He stacked the virtues in a deliberate order because the acquisition of one could facilitate the acquisition of another. Temperance, for example, would give him the coolness and clearness of head to produce vigilance and put off temptations that would hinder his efforts to attain the other virtues. Then silence would be easier – a virtue of which Franklin thought he had a particularly strong need. He believed that he made too many puns and jokes, making him only acceptable to lower company.

He was like a gardener, who does not attempt to kill all the weeds at once, but works on one bed at a time. In this way he would progress through his virtues checklist: "So I should have, I hoped, the encouraging pleasure of seeing on my pages the progress I made in virtue, by clearing successively my lines of their spots, till in the end, by a number of courses, I should be happy in viewing a clean book, after a thirteen weeks' daily examination."

Franklin put together perhaps a more comprehensive plan for productivity and moral improvement than anyone else of his time. But did it work? Franklin discusses the results of his experiments with characteristic honesty in his autobiography. Erasing his faults was not as easy as he believed it would be at first. But he did witness slow and steady progress: "I was supris'd to find myself so much fuller of faults that I had imagined," he said, "but I had the satisfaction of seeing them diminish."

His virtues cycle also went much slower in practice than it did in theory – his first full cycle of the 13 virtues, instead of taking 13 weeks, took a full year. And he only did this cycle once in several years, not four times a year as he originally supposed. Franklin's busy life of international business and foreign voyages cut into his program of piety. Trips to France, with all its wine, *bordellos*, and acquiescent middle-aged women, probably did the most damage.

But even too much virtue could become a vice. Franklin realized that never making jokes would make him insufferable company. Perfect character would come with the "inconvenience of being envied and hated." He concluded that a benevolent man should allow a few faults in himself in order to keep some friends. Oscar Wilde would have agreed with this sentiment a century later, noting that one should seek "moderation in all things, especially moderation."

He never arrived at perfection, but he was glad that he undertook the endeavor in the first place. Franklin credited attempts at Temperance to living to a ripe old age; to Industry and Frugality for earning his fortune; and to Sincerity and Justice for earning the confidence of his country. He writes that it was better to undertake the experiment and fall short than to not try at all. He was a better and happier man than he otherwise should have been.

To Franklin, becoming a perfect person was an impossible task, but a goal worth attempting anyway. Much like trying to hand-copy an engraved illustration, there will always be a flaw in any attempt. But with each pass, one's drawing ability improves. Franklin was never a perfect man, but as a statesman, inventor, entrepreneur, media mogul, and philosopher, he certainly achieved enough in his life to compensate for any flaws, particularly in the final years.

Franklin experienced a new burst of energy in his 70s. Deborah, his wife of 44 years, died in 1774, two years before he became the first U.S. ambassador to France. The 70-year-old arrived to France with an electrifying welcome. He was the best-known American in Europe due to his internationally famous scientific research. After settling in France, Franklin became an even bigger sensation due to his polyamorous ways and his wit, which the French perceived to be rustic New World genius. Franklin carried this pose to the extreme. When he was presented to the king, instead of wearing an expensive uniform, he wore a plain brown suit and carried his hat under his arm. He was often spotted in salon society wearing a coonskin cap.

This fit into the French notion of the Americans as some kind of a new race, purged of the fancy wigs and powdered hair of the Old World.

Franklin was soon a fixture among the French elite, including that of King Louis XVI. He charmed aristocratic society, using his uncanny knack for politics and persuasion to secure French financial and military aid for the Revolutionary War. His charm offensive is all the more remarkable considering his rudimentary understanding of the French language. He noted that a man expressing himself in a language not his own loses half his intellect. His command of the French language was so poor that a French professor in the 1950s graded Franklin's language usage. It wasn't good. Franklin earned an A- in oral comprehension, a B- in spoken French, and an F for his written skills. But despite these limitations he forged ahead. Franklin used his social gaffes and malapropisms to his advantage. He adopted the French style of working hard without appearing to be trying at all.

In addition to his ambassadorial duties, while in France Franklin also served as grand master of a freemason lodge in Paris from 1779 until 1781. He advocated religious tolerance to Louis, resulting in the king signing the Edict of Versailles in 1787, which ended the denial of non-Catholics civil status and the right to openly practice their faith. When he left his residence of Passy, a small town outside of Paris in which he resided, Thomas Jefferson wrote that "it seemed as if the village had lost its patriarch."

Franklin returned to America in 1785. He took up the role of elder statesman, championing the cause of liberty in the young country. He freed his two slaves and became president of the Pennsylvania Abolition Society. Franklin then served for three years as the leader of Pennsylvania, in a position equivalent to governor, from 1785 to 1788. Not resting on his laurels, Franklin served as a delegate to the Philadelphia Convention in 1787, becoming the only Founding Father to sign the Declaration of Independence, the

Treaty of Alliance with France, the Treaty of Paris, and the United States Constitution. Following this period, he wrote several essays stressing the importance of the abolition of slavery as Congress endlessly debated the issue.

He made the most of all the years of his life, even his final years, when many settled for retirement and idleness. He maintained his curiosity, even as an elderly man, and never stopped learning. To Franklin, this was the proudest of his many accomplishments. It was the never-ending journey of discovery that propelled him forward until his death at age 84. He summed up this belief in a memorable quote before his death: "Being ignorant is not so much a shame, as being unwilling to learn."

CHAPTER FOUR

THOMAS EDISON (1847-1931)

Mark Twain, the most American of American writers, had few kind words to spare for Thomas Edison. To him, the inventor – arguably the most prolific inventor in all of history, with 1,093 patents to his name – was little more than a man who happened to be at the right place at the right time.

Of Edison he said:

It takes a thousand men to invent a telegraph, or a steam engine, or a phonograph, or a photograph, or a telephone or any other important thing—and the last man gets the credit and we forget the others. He added his little mite — that is all he did. These object lessons should teach us that ninety-nine parts of all things that proceed from the intellect are plagiarisms, pure and simple; and the lesson ought to make us modest. But nothing can do that.

Edison would have agreed that many of his inventions were improvements on what came before. But if we are to take Twain at his word, then we would have to believe that Edison had the blind luck to be at the right place at the right time *hundreds and hundreds of times* throughout his life. Edison's laboratory in Menlo Park, New Jersey, churned out new inventions so quickly that it mimicked a factory production schedule. It was so productive that at one point Edison promised to turn out a minor invention every 10 days and a big thing every six months or so.

He largely made good on his promise. Edison is responsible for inventing the practical incandescent light bulb, phonograph, motion picture camera, cement-making technology, batteries, and the electric power generation system. While Edison purchased and even stole some of these patents, nearly 100 percent of them were led to commercial success and quickly influenced American technological life.

More recent writers have vilified Edison as evil incarnate, a man who sued people out of business, slandered his competitors, and destroyed greater inventors such as Nikola Tesla. For example, he is commonly believed to have invented the light bulb, which he did not. Twenty-two other inventors pioneer the light bulb before him. But Edison gets credit because he was able to develop an incandescent light bulb that was cheap and did not burn out quickly.

Matthew Inman, creator of the web comic *The Oatmeal*, casts him as the worst villain in modern America. He said, "Edison, not skipping a beat when the opportunity to be awful presented itself, got to work right away on human trials in X-ray experimentation. One of his employees, Clarence Dally, was exposed to so much radiation that his arms had to be amputated to save his life. It didn't work though, and he eventually died from mediastinal cancer."

While Edison's star shines much less brightly than it did a few decades ago, when America considered him the embodiment of the tinkerer-genius. His bad reputation is a bit undeserved. First, both

Edison and his assistant who died from his X-ray human trials did not really understand how radiation worked and how dangerous it was. Edison also volunteered for the experiment and suffered from excessive dosage, like Marie and Pierre Curie.

Second, whatever he may have lacked as a scientific genius, his productivity still cannot be dismissed. He produced inventions on a scale that was 10 or even 100 times greater than his closest competitors. Tesla was a brilliant futurist and inventor of the induction motor, but he could not match Edison in terms of output. Edison had over 1,000 patents to his name. thanks to a research lab full of assistants who carried out mundane details of his projects. This output stands in stark contrast to that of Tesla, who preferred to work alone and do everything himself, and filed "only" 112 patents over the course of his life.

Thomas Alva Edison was born on February 11, 1847, in Ohio. He didn't attend public school for long due to his short attention span and non-conformist streak. His mother, a former school teacher, homeschooled him instead during his primary and secondary school years. Edison was largely self-taught and devoured books from the local library. He was not afraid of hard work, whether as a curious adolescent or inventor. "Genius is all bosh," he told *The New York Sun* in 1878. "Clean hard work is what does the business."

One friend who had known the inventor since he was 14, claimed on his own knowledge that Edison never spent an idle day in his life. Often when he should have been asleep, he was known to sit up half the night reading. He did not read novels or Western adventures popular among boys in the late 19th century, preferring books on mechanics, chemistry, and electricity, which his friend claimed that Edison mastered at this young age.

At the age of 12, Edison got a job selling newspapers on a train route that ran through Port Huron. Soon he obtained the exclusive rights to sell newspapers between Port Huron and Detroit, the first of his early business successes. But to acknowledge Mr. Twain, this and other turns in Edison's story can be attributed partially to luck. At age 16 he saved the life of Jimmie MacKenzie from an oncoming train. The young man was the son of a telegraph operator, who rewarded Edison by training him in this skill, a prestigious job at the time. Knowledge of telegraphy was a technical skill that would serve as a gateway to phonography and the telephone. It also taught him knowledge of the fundamentals of electricity, the foundation of nearly all his later inventions.

He filed his first patent in Boston in 1869 at the age of 22. His first invention was the electrical vote recorder. The invention intended to speed up the process of recording votes for the Massachusetts state legislature. There was only one problem – local politicians had no interest in speeding up the vote count. They feared it would hurt the procedure of vote trading and maneuvering, crucial for the political process. Edison realized that he found a solution in need of a problem., an important lesson for the budding inventor. His products needed to match the needs of the market. An invention with little practical utility would be ignored and never enter mass production. From this beginning he began to evolve into the hybrid inventor-CEO that defined his career.

Another explanation for Edison's productivity was his ability to turn the dullest of life's moments into an opportunity to work. When he was 19, he took a job running the Associated Press news wire during the night shift. He took this unwanted job because so little happened that he could perform experiments at his work bench. Edison tested new inventions while "working" at his job for several months, with his supervisors unaware. Something finally happened that could not go unnoticed. One day he was experimenting with batteries and spilled sulfuric acid on the floor. It leaked through the floor boards and onto his boss's desk the floor below. The youth was fired the next day.

He invented the phonograph in 1877. The device seemed magical to the public, earning him the name "The Wizard of Menlo Park." He became a celebrity. The next year Edison travelled to Washington to demonstrate the phonograph to Congressmen, Senators, and President Rutherford B. Hayes. He then used funds from the sale of his quadruplex telegraph to build an industrial research laboratory. Based in Menlo Park, New Jersey it was one of the first institutions created for the specific purpose of technological innovation instead of theoretical research. This lab was the forefather of similar research labs at Intel, General Electric, and AT&T.

Once he had his own laboratory, Edison created a sophisticated operation with intelligent employees. Edison's organizational abilities allowed him to develop his creative designs, pass them on to assistants, and multiply his effectiveness far beyond what he could do personally. He could institutionalize his work ethic at an organizational level.

But Edison did not accomplish results merely by outsourcing designs to staff. He was famous for his dogged determinism and rarely demoralized by a failed experiment. Sarah Knowles Bolton wrote in 1885 that when one of his inventions, a printing machine, failed, he took five men into the loft of his factory and declared he would not come down until it worked satisfactorily. For over two days and nights – 60 hours total – he worked without sleep. Edison then conquered the problem and rewarded himself with 30 hours of rest.

Other failures approached a level so epic that they were barely outmatched by his successes. Among his most spectacular failures was the electric pen. Edison created it to meet the demand of railroad companies who needed their administrators to quickly make multiple copies of handwritten documents. It was powered by a battery and small electric motor and relied on a needle that punched tiny holes in paper. The idea was for an employee to stencil a document on wax paper and make copies by rolling ink over it, creating essentially a miniature printing press. But few wanted to spend $30 (more than a week's wages) on a device that was noisy and powered by a battery that had to be maintained in a chemical solution. It wasn't a total failure, though: some consider his electric pen the forefather of the tattoo needle. Historians of science don't know whether the needle came directly from his electrical pen or it was a convergent evolution, but the two devices bear an uncanny resemblance.

Another great failure in 1890 was a good idea but too far ahead of its time: the talking doll. This was among his first inventions that was planned to be designed in a short time and quickly manufactured and turned into a fast profit. He placed a small phonograph inside German dolls. But customers returned them almost immediately. They said the dolls were too fragile for children and would break with the slightest bump. Plus, the voices sounded garbled and haunting. Edison took them off the market after a month.

He took pride in these missteps. "I have not failed 10,000 times – I've successfully found 10,000 ways that will not work," he said. According to the Smithsonian magazine profile of Leonard DeGraaf, archivist at the Thomas Edison National Historical Park, the inventor stood out because his fearlessness in the face of failure and refusal to dwell on mistakes. Since Edison had thousands of other inventions under his belt, he did not depend on one thing or think too long about his botched ideas. DeGraaf wrote, "Even for his biggest failures he didn't spend a lot of time wringing his hands and saying 'Oh my God, we spent a fortune on that.' Instead he said, 'We had fun spending it.'"

This perseverance allowed Edison to complete designs that refused to cooperate on the first, second, or hundredth try. Aside from the mass-market incandescent light bulb, his greatest invention was the phonograph, which he introduced in 1888.

The phonograph took nearly a decade to bring to the market. He first conceived of the idea in the 1870s of turning electromagnetic waves into speech using grooved paper disks or spools of paper tape, and eventually settling on a tinfoil disk. In his first experiment he cranked a handle and spoke "Mary Had a Little Lamb" into the machine, as it traced grooves onto the disk. He returned it to the starting point and cranked it again, hearing his voice echo back to him.

Although news of his success was a media sensation the only potential buyers appeared to be scientists or collectors of novelty items. Plus, tinfoil was so delicate it could only be played once or twice before becoming unusable. Edison spent 10 years testing every substance imaginable until settling on the wax cylinder. Then, his invention succeeded dramatically and became the dominant audio recording format for most of the 20th century. Records were only displaced by CDs in the 1980s. A small number of photographs and phonograph records are still produced today.

His laboratory in Menlo Park was famous for having in stock nearly every conceivable material. The field of material sciences did not exist in those days, and researchers often had to use trial and error to determine how different materials reacted with each other. So Edison's materials supply items included over 8,000 kinds of chemicals, every size of needle, every kind of screw made, every kind of cord or wire, hair of humans, horses, hogs, cows, rabbits, goats, minx, camels, silk in every texture, cocoons, various kinds of hoofs, shark teeth, deer horns, tortoise shells, cork, resin, varnish and oil, ostrich feathers, a peacock's tail, and all forms of ores.

Edison's research laboratory had a large machine shop and a precision machine shop. There were separate laboratories to study chemistry, electricity, and metallurgy. There was space for manufacturing and a recording studio. All were illuminated by Edison's incandescent lights, allowing for progress to continue unabated at all hours.

And with Edison at the helm, it likely did continue at all hours. One explanation of Edison's profligacy is his strange sleep schedule. In a 1901 interview, journalist Orison Swett Mardsen asked the famous inventor a number of questions about his sleeping habits. Edison first dismissed rest as a waste of time and "a heritage from our cave days." The 53-year-old then responded with a detailed account of his daily routine, admitting he had slowed down compared to his work schedule as a young man: "I come to the laboratory at about 8 o'clock every day and go home to tea at six, and then I study and work at some problem until 11, which is my hour for bed." When the interviewer responded that a 14 or 15-hour work schedule could scarcely be called loafing, Edison responded, "Well, for 15 years, I worked on average of 20 hours a day." He even claimed that when he was 47 years old, he estimated his true age at 82 because of all the hours he gained by not devoting them to sleep.

He was so dismissive of sleep that he wrote the following in 1921.

People will not only do what they like to do — they overdo it 100 percent. Most people overeat 100 percent, and oversleep 100 percent, because they like it. That extra 100 percent makes them unhealthy and inefficient. The person who sleeps eight or ten hours a night is never fully asleep and never fully awake — they have only different degrees of dozing through the twenty-four hours. ... For myself I never found need of more than four or five hours' sleep in the twenty-four. I never dream. It's real sleep. When by chance I have taken more, I wake dull and indolent. We are always hearing people talk about 'loss of sleep' as a calamity. They better call it loss of time, vitality and opportunities. Just to satisfy my curiosity I have gone through files of the British Medical Journal and could not find a single case reported of anybody being hurt by loss of sleep. Insomnia is different entirely — but some people think they have insomnia if they can sleep only ten hours every night.

Edison liked to boast that he only slept three or four hours a night – and even claimed that he would have marathon inventing sessions 72 hours long. However, the truth about his relationship with somnolence was more complicated. Edison had a cot in his office and would frequently steal power naps. He got close to a normal amount of sleep, but broke it up throughout the day instead of a single stretch. Napping cots were scattered throughout his vast property, tucked away in libraries and labs. One day his friend Henry Ford paid a visit. Edison's assistant told him that he couldn't enter his office because the famed inventor was snoozing. "But I thought Edison didn't sleep very much." His assistant answered, "He doesn't sleep very much at all, he just naps a lot."

Edison was capable of entering deep sleep almost anywhere at any time. Such locations included his workbench or in a closet. He typically snuck in one or two 3-hour naps during the day, sleeping "as sound as a bug in a barrel of morphine." In one famous photograph he is shown napping under a tree at the Ford Edison Camp in Hagerstown, Maryland. Behind him are seated President Warren Harding and tire magnate Harvey Firestone, both chatting casually and reading the newspaper as the inventor is stretched out on the grass.

Once Edison awoke from these naps, he would immediately resume his work, ready to leap into another experiment. Numerous accounts state he awoke reinvigorated, with no mental fog or grogginess. Authors Frank Lewis Dyer and Thomas Martin wrote that after Edison threw himself down on a cot and fell into instantaneous sleep, he always awoke immediately and "in full possession of his faculties, arising from the cot and going 'back to the job' without a moment's hesitation."

His life was lived in the lab. Edison gave complete time and mental energy to his experiments. Because of his intense focus on work, he had a poor family life. His first wife rarely saw him. Their relationship languished until she died in 1884 at the age of 29 due to a morphine overdose. (Her doctors had prescribed morphine as a treatment for disease). His son, Thomas Jr., had such a poor relationship with his father that he dropped the Edison surname and used a number of aliases. The elder Edison cut off relations with one of his daughters for marrying a German officer, considered to be a shameful act in the patriotic days of World War I-era America.

Ironically, Edison's extreme work habits may have made him less effective an inventor than he ultimately could have been. Edison was so well known for throwing hundreds of hours at a project that his critics accused him of working with gross inefficiency, without regard to forethought or an ounce of theory. Upon Edison's death, Nikola Tesla wrote the following.

> He had no hobby, cared for no sort of amusement of any kind and lived in utter disregard of the most elementary rules of hygiene... his method was inefficient in the extreme, for an immense ground had to be covered to get anything at all unless blind chance intervened and, at first, I was almost a sorry witness of his doings, knowing that just a little theory and calculation would have saved him 90% of the labor. But he had a veritable contempt for book learning and mathematical knowledge, trusting himself entirely to his inventor's instinct and practical American sense.

Edison would have likely not disagreed with Tesla's assessment because he never claimed to be a research scientist. He was less concerned with scientific breakthroughs in the lab, which often remained confined to academic journals, and more concerned if his ideas could be brought to market. "I am not a scientific man. I am an inventor," he told the *Brooklyn Citizen* in 1888. "As soon as I find that something I am investigating does not lead to practical results, I do not pursue it as theory."

The inventor also denied that the key to success in life was working 18 hours a day, regardless of how those 18 hours were spent. Most men put in 16 good hours a day, Edison said. They have either been walking or reading or writing or thinking. But they do it about a great many different things. The difference with him, he said, is that he did it about only one thing. If an average man took the time in question and applied it to one direction, to one object, he would succeed. The trouble rested in the fact that people did not have an object, one thing, to which they stuck, letting all else go. Success, he said, is the product of the severest kind of mental and physical application.

If this maxim is true, few applied it as well as Edison.

CHAPTER FIVE

ELON MUSK (1971-)

Director Jon Favreau was busy preparing for the 2008 release of the movie Iron Man, but he had a major problem. Scriptwriters weren't able to make the character of genius billionaire Tony Stark appear realistic. They worried that a technological wunderkind playboy would fail to make the transition from the comics and look too cartoonish onscreen. Favreau finally took Robert Downey Jr.'s suggestion to meet with a man who was as close to a real-life Tony Stark as they could hope to find.

They shook hands with a tall, energetic engineer who was also the founder of an electric car company and rocket ship firm. After their meeting with Elon Musk concluded, Favreau was able to make the script fall quickly into place. He called Musk "a paragon of enthusiasm, good humor and curiosity – a Renaissance man in an era that needs them."

The 43-year-old native South African is CEO of SpaceX, the first private rocket company able to send payloads to the

International Space Station. On top of that he is the CEO and chief product architect of Tesla Motors, which has produced a line of electric cars since 2008. Despite the cost of the cars running into the six figures, there is a months-long waiting list. He sells thousands of its Model S sedans per month and claims Tesla will sell a few million cars by 2025. If so, Musk will fulfill the dream of making electric cars a mass-market reality, which other car makers have failed to accomplish for over a century. (Have electric cars been produced for over a century?)

Musk's ability to achieve exceptional feats of productivity began after his immigration to the United States in the 1990s. He created and sold the software company Zip2 for $300 million, receiving 7% of the sale. Then he joined a humble startup called PayPal and sold it to eBay three years later for $1.5 billion.

Living as one of the idle rich wasn't enough for Musk. He then resolved to fix two problems. First, he would replace the internal combustion engine with a global fleet of electric cars. Next, he would build dependable, reusable rockets that would make the cost of spaceflight drop by a factor of 10. Humanity would be able to easily reach Earth's orbit and perhaps even colonize Mars.

But Musk's path to success did not follow a linear trajectory. Following the financial crash in 2008, Tesla was near bankruptcy after a financing round fell through. Banks were no longer handing out capital to unproven industries. Also, Tesla was in a lawsuit with former employees. Musk put over $200 million of his own money into all his ventures, nearly depleting his savings. He came close to personal bankrupty after a divorce and had to borrow money from friends for living expenses.

SpaceX was also in danger of shutting its doors. Its first rocket, the Falcon 1, cost $100 million to produce. The rocket stood nearly 70 feet tall and could carry a payload to orbit of up to 1,256 pounds. But its first two launches ended in explosion. The first launch in 2006 ended with a fuel line leak and fire; the second in 2007 nearly reached orbital velocity before the rocket's second stage engine shut down because of roll control issues and fuel slosh. At the third launch in 2008, Musk was under extreme pressure. He told the press a few years earlier that he might have to admit defeat if SpaceX couldn't be successful three launches in.

On August 2, 2008, a Falcon 1 rocket launched from the U.S. Army's Reagan Test Site on Melek Island in the Kwajalein Atoll, located about 2,500 miles southwest of Hawaii in the Pacific Ocean. The launch team watched the video transmission with bated breath. Suddenly, the transmission terminated. After the first stage flight, immediately following separation when the first stage detaches from the second stage and falls way, the two stages collided. The rocket exploded heading back to earth in pieces. The payload of three NASA satellites was incinerated during orbital re-entry.

Musk composed himself, walked past the press, and addressed the 350 employees who had worked 80+ hours a week for six years. Everyone looked at him with graveyard silence. They had struggled against giants in the aerospace industry, limits of technology, politics, lobbying, and financial difficulties. Now their business looked ready to close.

Musk reacted to catastrophe by offering inspiration. According to an account by Dolly Singh, Musk's former head of talent acquisition, Musk told the crowd that everyone knew this was going to be hard, as it is, after all, rocket science. He listed off the half-dozen countries which had failed to successfully execute even a first-stage launch and get to outer space, which SpaceX had successfully done that day. But he let them know that the possibility of failure had been taken into account, and he acquired a significant investment from Draper Fischer Jurveston, allowing for at least another launch. He then told everyone to pick themselves up and dust themselves off.

Singh said, "Then, with as much fortitude and ferocity as he could muster after having been awake for like 20+ hours, he said,

'For my part I will never give up and *I mean never*,' and he said that if we would stick with him, we will win."

"I think most of us would have followed him into the gates of hell carrying suntan oil after that," she said.

Within seconds the entire work force transformed into a hive of energy. Within a matter of hours the SpaceX team identified the cause of launch failure, a process usually taking weeks or months. Within 7 weeks another rocket was fully manufactured, integrated, and ready to fly again – which normally takes 6 months.

On September 28, 2008, SpaceX prepared for its fourth launch. If it had not succeeded, the company would have closed. But the fourth launch did succeed. The Falcon 1 flew from Kwajalein Atoll in the South Pacific into the atmosphere, becoming the first privately-funded rocket to achieve Earth orbit.

The legend of Musk's productivity goes beyond his ability to inspire others around him. His work schedule is as compact and efficiently engineered as any one of his rockets. He routinely works 80-100 hours per week, pushing the upper ceiling of what a human can accomplish in the weekly allotment of 168 hours. But somehow he did even more in the early days of the 2008 financial crisis.

He has talked with the media numerous times about his daily schedule. At one point, he said, "It's really varied over time. These days it's probably 80, 85 hours a week. For awhile there it was over 100 hours a week. And that's just… it's just too… that's a very high amount of pain. The difficulty in pain of work hours really increases exponentially; it's not linear. When the financial crisis hit in 2008, 2009, it was every day, seven days a week, morning till night and then dream about work. Just terrible."

The day starts for Musk at 7 am. He usually skips breakfast, devours lunch in five minutes during a meeting, and occasionally exercises. Apart from work, that's about it. Monday, he's at SpaceX in Los Angeles. Tuesday and Wednesday, Tesla in Palo Alto. Thursday and Friday, back at SpaceX. Despite the physical and mental toll of this schedule, Musk would recommend it to others if they want to succeed: "If other people are putting in 40 hour work weeks and you're putting in 100-hour work weeks, then even if you're doing the same thing you know that... you will achieve in 4 months what it takes them a year to achieve."

He squeezes as much as possible out of each day due to a laser-like focus on productivity. Musk fires out hundreds of one or two-word emails a day instead of conducting meetings. He constantly questions what does and doesn't work, always paring back the latter. "I think it's very important to have a feedback loop, where you're constantly thinking about what you've done and how you could be doing it better. I think that's the single best piece of advice: constantly think about how you could be doing things better and questioning yourself."

He has applied this lesson to himself by taking on the steep learning curve required by designing the SpaceX. Musk taught himself the physics of rocketry in order to design its first rocket, the Falcon 1, along with the Falcon 9 booster. He did this despite never designing anything apart from rocket models as a child. Musk did not initially intend to be the chief design of the rocket. "But the people who were willing to join early on weren't up to the task and the people that were weren't willing to join. So I ended up by default becoming the chief rocket designer, which obviously has its plusses and minuses."

Beyond squeezing in triple-digit hours of work per week, Musk's level of productivity comes from traits shared by Thomas Edison. Both had incredible work ethics while they are on the job. They spent nearly every waking hour in their offices. If they were not in the office physically, they were there mentally. Musk accomplishes this by questionable means. He told an audience at a 2013 South by Southwest panel that he responds to email while interacting with his children. He argues that his five children are young enough that they do not require his undivided attention, and he can talk to them and answer short emails at the same time.

"Kids are awesome," he said to the audience. "You guys should all have kids ... I don't see mine enough actually. But what I find is I'm able to be with them and still be on email. I can be with them and still be working at the same time ... If I didn't, I wouldn't be able to get my job done." Responses were mostly negative to his take on parenting, which was interpreted by the audience as an attempt to justify neglect.

A more important characteristic that Musk shares with Edison is resilience in the face of obstacles. When looking at a risky proposition, Musk acknowledges the likelihood of failure, but does not use it as final criteria of whether or not a goal should be pursued. His employees had hundreds of anecdotes to back this up. Roshan Thomas was one of the first employees at Tesla, joining a middle management position in 2001. He said that during his interview he asked Musk when he embarks on a project, whether or not the huge hurdles or high barriers to entry give him pause? The CEO answered that he looked at two things before embarking on anything: 1) Can it be done? Are we breaking any laws of physics? 2) Is it important enough for humanity that it would make a major dent? If the answer to 1 and 2 is 'yes,' then he would move forward.

For example, when he first shopped around to see if he could purchase a Russian intercontinental ballistic missile for his nascent Mars company, his dealer kept changing the price on him. He looked to American launch companies, but the cost was $60-80 million. Instead of finding a cheap supplier, he decided to create his own rocket company.

SpaceX ultimately found success when it signed a $1.6 billion contract with NASA and purchased a 20-year lease on a launch pad in Cape Canaveral, but there are still obstacles to overcome. In 2014, Musk bought a tract of land in Texas to build a dedicated spaceport for SpaceX. Approval from all government agencies took years, as if federal bureaucrats were determined to sabotage the project. "There were a million federal agencies that needed to sign off, and the final call went to the National Historic Landmark Association, because the last battle of the Civil War was fought a few miles away from our site, and visitors *might* be able to see the tip of our rocket from there. We were like, 'Really? Have you seen what it's like around there? Nobody visits that place.'"

Musk is motivated to work so hard because he is motivated by his work – a tautological statement, but one that has a bearing on how he spends his day. He has resolved to spend so much time on a private rocket company not because he thinks that good money can be found in the aerospace industry but because he ultimately wants to settle humans on Mars as a species insurance policy. His long term goal is to colonize the Red Planet with tens of thousands of pioneers, establish a permanent settlement, and even retire there. With humanity as an interplanetary species, the light of consciousness would continue to glow even if an asteroid wiped out all of Earth's life. Musk argues that steady progress amidst failure is to truly believe in the importance of your task. "If something is important enough," he said, "even if the odds are against you, you should do it."

Some of his more futuristic concepts resemble technology found in a Ray Bradbury novel. In 2013 he unveiled a proposal for transportation system between Los Angeles and San Francisco. Dubbed the "Hyperloop," it is a subsonic air travel machine that will stretch 350 miles between the two cities, allowing a commuter to travel between the two in less than 30 minutes at speeds of 800 miles an hour, faster than a commercial airplane and much faster than the California High-Speed rail system currently under construction. The Hyperloop system will be fully enclosed and uses a partial vacuum to reduce aerodynamic drag, theoretically allowing high speed at low power. The cost is estimated to be $6 billion. Musk assigned dozens of engineers from SpaceX and Tesla to establish the conceptual foundations. He then handed it off to a private group of engineers to fill in the details. Musk is planning to build a 5-mile test track for the Hyperloop system in Texas to establish proof of concept.

The Hyperloop may never see the light of day, but it is an example of Musk's unwillingness to be confined by the status quo. He calls this "first principles" thinking. It is a thought process that allows a designer to innovate in clear leaps instead of incremental gains. The normal approach to solving a problem is by analogy, constricting a solution based on what has been done before or what others are doing. With first principles thinking, an innovator begins at the most fundamental truths and reasons from there. This process requires more mental energy, but it allows for startling innovation.

It is a unique approach to productivity. Take the design of the Tesla Model S. Musk is obsessed with each car being perfect. At one time he personally looked at every car, did a visual inspection, and drove one or two at random. He noticed in one test that the installation of the headlamp was not quite correct. There was a 3-millimeter asymmetry between the right and the left. He discovered that the lead tech was still operating with the part dimensions of an old part. After that episode he told the whole assembly that they were empowered to be perfectionists on the line. They should not let a car pass their station if anything is wrong. They must reverse the line and send it back.

Musk has told his teams that he wanted the cars to be so accurate that they could be used as a calibration device. If he wanted to know how long a meter was, he could measure the car. Musk wants them to be accurate to the limit of reasonable physics. In the future Tesla will order laser calibration devices to calibrate the car within tenths of a millimeter. This approach to design accuracy literally comes from the design book for rocket design. "This is very extreme for the car business, but for the rocket business it is not, so from my standpoint, when people say you can't do that, it's like, 'I do that every day. What are you talking about? I know it's possible.' We're trying to take the precision of rockets, where fractions of a millimeter can mean the difference between success and failure. We're applying rocket science to the car business. If you want to make the best car, that's what you have to do."

The final key to Musk's productivity is setting high expectations for his employees. He makes it known to new factory techs that they will work more hours than a regular job. Forty-hour weeks are for those looking for safety, not for innovation. "If you work for Tesla, the minimum is really a 50-hour week, and there are times when it'll be 60 to 80-hour weeks. The general understanding is that if you're at Tesla, you're choosing to be at the equivalent of the Special Forces. There's the regular Army, and that's fine, but if you are working at Tesla, you're choosing to step up your game."

PART II

WRITERS AND ARTISTS

CHAPTER SIX

LEONARDO DA VINCI (1452-1519)

Few Renaissance figures have as many legends swirling around their life as Leonardo da Vinci. The first is that he developed a flying machine centuries before the Wright Brothers (an idea taken to a comically ridiculous extreme in an episode of *Futurama*, where da Vinci is revealed to be an extraterrestrial whose devices are capable of interstellar travel). Second, according to *The Da Vinci Code*, he revealed clues to the "true" lineage of Jesus in his paintings.

The myths persist because of the unconventional nature of his life. Leonardo was a painter, architect, sculptor, mathematician, engineer, musician, inventor, anatomist, geologist, botanist, cartographer, military strategist, and writer. Leonardo is the ideal of a multi-accomplished humanist figure, meaning that he had confidence in the ability of humans to determine for themselves truth and falsehood. He employed unusual empirical methods of the time to approach his broad scope of interest. He made discoveries in optics, hydrodynamics, engineering, and anatomy. He conceived of flying machines, armored vehicles, calculators, the double hull, and even concentrated solar power. Few of his designs came to fruition – his flying machine would have crashed into the ground if ever built and tested – but some of his designs were manufactured, such as a machine that tested the tensile strength of wire and an automated bobbin winder.

Leonardo's talents were so great that many modern critics fault him with not accomplishing even more in his life. He was widely known for his poor work habits and terrible procrastination. Although he filled sketch books with examinations and theories, he never edited, organized, or published them, leaving their discovery for the 19th century. His ideas, furthermore, have no mathematical foundation and are more doodling than any sort of challenge to Isaac Newton. Algebra was unknown to him and he was below-average at figures. Leonardo preferred visual observation rather than data-driven analysis. J. Wisniewski writes that given Leonardo's long working life and poor attention span, his brilliance defies explanation: "Imagine LeBron James playing a dozen sports, giving each up after a few months before playing a single season in the NBA and averaging 50 points a game per game...only to retire and take up butterfly collecting."

Despite these criticisms – which may not be fair considering that Leonardo depended on patronage for completing his projects and had to have diverse interests by necessity – there are many lessons to take from his life about productivity. He is for good reason the ideal Renaissance man. His 7,000 pages of notes filled with dubious science notwithstanding, Leonardo's perceptive powers to see and notice in a way that nobody had ever done before makes his observations thrilling.

Leonardo found early success by aligning himself with power. He had to learn this lesson quickly. He was the bastard child of a poor farm girl, had no formal education, and would have languished in obscurity if not for the help of a powerful patron. Although children born out of wedlock were rarely able to enter elite circles in 15th-century Italy, Leonardo decided that his pathway forward ran through the Medici, a powerful banking family, political dynasty, and royal house. As a teenager he traveled to Florence and built relations with the most well-regarded artists in the Italian peninsula. He took an apprenticeship in the famed studio of Andrea del Verrocchio at the age of 15. His skills as an artist developed and flourished to the point of intimidating his mentor. At the age of 20, he was accepted into the Painters' Guild of Florence, giving him access to prestigious merchants, politicians, and religious figures. He then moved to Milan and offered his services to Duke Ludovico Sforza as a military engineer. Here he began to develop many of his famous military inventions.

Leonardo would have been an even more prolific creator if not for his incessant perfectionism. Few artists made the perfect as much of the enemy of the good as he did. He struggled to finish paintings because accepting a standard of only perfection meant that he often abandoned projects out of frustration or boredom. He rarely finished what he began unless it was a project for an extraordinarily wealthy patron. It took Leonardo 25 years to finish the "Virgin on the Rocks." His masterpiece "Mona Lisa" took nearly 15 years.

Fra Pietro di Novellara, the vicar general of the Carmelite Order, wrote a 1501 letter to Isabella d'Este of Mantua to explain to her why her painting commissioned to Leonardo was delayed: "His mathematical experiments have so estranged him from painting that he cannot bear to take up the brush." His contemporaries could not understand how an artist could trifle with scientific experiments – considered far less estimable at the time – and a distraction from the more practical matters of artistic creation. They considered Leonardo's scientific sketches on anatomy only worthy to be treasured as relics.

Historian Kenneth Keele, who has examined Da Vinci's sketches of anatomy, considered what it meant for Leonardo to be chained to

15th-century errors in his research because there was no support system of knowledge to buffet his ideas.

At every page I am fascinated by his intelligent questions and answers. But I often find myself realizing that however intelligent, however full of instinctive weight the questions are, if the supporting base of knowledge is not there the answers are bound to contain errors. This makes my tale inevitably one tinged with sadness; and the more Leonardo struggles within his chains of ignorance the sadder it becomes. Especially is this so because though he breaks his fetters in many places he never escapes from them. I wonder if in a number of fields (I would cite sociology, psychology, thanatology) we are not in a rather similarly sad state today with the fetters being no less powerful for being unknown to us, even unfelt.

For these reasons Leonardo cannot be blamed for many of his unfinished many of his projects. His scale of ambition was so high – a systemization of all knowledge of nature – that his inventions exceeded the instruments, experimental methods, and mathematics available at the time. Since he could not know which directions would lead to success, he struck out in all of them at the same time. Despite his many failures, modern historians and researchers are fascinated to the degree he was able to achieve and conceive. He grasped inventions that lacked any supporting knowledge or technology of the era. Some of his speculative war machines included the 33-barreled organ, a multi-barreled gun that could be loaded and fired simultaneously, a precursor to the modern machine gun; the armored car, a tank-like device covered with a turtle-shell-like protective top and equipped with a number of light cannons arranged on a circular platform with wheels that allowed for 360 degrees of range; and the giant crossbow, which measured 27 yards across and would fire massive stones or flaming bombs at an awestruck enemy.

His ideas were so far ahead of their time that they sometimes appeared to be nonsense. Early in his career Leonardo submitted sketches to the Royal Palace of Milan of a mechanical device capable of firing heavy projectiles and an accompanying device that could deter such fire. He signed his letter as "a genius designer of weapons in war." The sketches looked remarkably similar to cannons and tanks, not used until 400 years later in the First World War. The prince did not know what to make of these alien devices. He was looking at the designs of a man too far ahead of his time, who, Freud observed was "like a man who awoke too early in the darkness, while the others were all still asleep."

But in him we see early glimpses of a modern mind. A key to his productivity is challenging assumptions. As an early Renaissance man, he both respected ancient sources but eschewed dependence on them at the same time. No matter that Aristotle said this or that about natural principles, Leonardo preferred to test nature itself: "Those who study the ancients and not the works of Nature are stepsons and not sons of Nature, the mother of all good authors," he said. Leonardo tested the principles of Aristotle, Ptolemy and Galen. He believed that nature followed pure mathematical principles and used mathematical proportions in his art. Leonardo argued that the human body was based on these proportions and wrote in the margins of an anatomical study, "Let no one read me who is not a mathematician."

It must be noted that Leonardo was by no means a modern scientist. His ideas used classical Greek thought as his frame of reference for experimentation. Leonardo's astronomy was largely Ptolemaic and his physiology Galenic. He worked within the late medieval tradition of an artisan, in which his patron called on him to do many practical things, whether diverting the flow of a stream, building defensive walls, or painting a picture. His profession blended the jobs of the mechanic, sculptor, artist, and architect. Some of the writings that he left behind to us include a system of movable barricades to protect the city of Venice from attack and a scheme of diverting the flow of the Arno River. While modern thinkers have credited him with being a man ahead of his time for combining science and technology when nobody else did, this is an anachronism. Leonardo rarely focused on the theory of *how* he made inventions but rather delved into tinkering to determine *if* it could be done.

But what cannot be denied is that he is memorable for blending gifts together. Many of his contemporaries were gifted painters or craftsmen, but few excelled at both trades to the level of Leonardo. His blending of gifts makes his wonderful sketches of flying machines and human physiology so memorable. He was at least recognized in his lifetime for artistic accomplishment. He lived in an era when artistic achievement was considered to be the glory of princes and subjects alike. A generation after Leonardo, Giorgio Vasari said of him that he was "truly admirable indeed, and divinely endowed. He might have been a scientist if he had not been so versatile. But the instability of his character caused him to take up and abandon many things."

There are glimpses of an organized mind in all the chaos. Leonardo had his own unique organizational system. He used a rudimentary form of planning in which ideas are visualized and broken down into their constituent parts. Known as "mind mapping," it is a popular form of planning by business leaders today. In his notebooks, Leonardo connected drawings and words in a flowing tree-like branch structure. It is a more dynamic form than classical outlining, which used roman numerals, topics, and subtopics.

He sketched his ideas starting with a central idea in the middle, then drawing out connections to other images and ideas that flowed from the central thesis. From these sub-ideas branched out other ideas and concepts, as deeply as the planner wants to go. Leonardo was free of the linear constraints of traditional techniques, allowing for new ideas to fit seamlessly within the structure and for the larger idea to evolve with the process rather than be constricted by a rigid initial outline. He could brainstorm easily with this technique, whether on the steps to complete a defensive wall, the elements of human anatomy, or parts of a mechanical crossbow.

Leonardo's method of planning came from his approach to rational inquiry. He considered everything to be connected to everything else. His integration of artistry and words opened him up to a much more creative approach than a traditional list would allow. He could brainstorm on the fly, tweak his ideas, and pile on new approaches without disturbing the basic structure. While Leonardo did not originate the concept of mind-mapping – Porphyry of Tyre did it in 4th century Greece and it remained a popular approach in medieval Arabia – he utilized it to a highly effective degree in his approach to art, inventions, or mechanics.

The artist could have never known it, but mind-mapping has support from neuroscience for planning over a traditional bullet-point outline. Studies of the brain show that visual images are processed and recalled better than written ones. A skeletal outline structure will come to the mind faster than Roman numerals. Drawing and connecting images triggers creative parts of the brain. Sketching out ideas with a central concept in the middle and drawing connections to other images that flow from the central idea allows one to map out concepts in a faster and more natural way. It even resembles a map of the brain, where synapses and neurons weave trillions of connections in a complex matrix but manage to produce elegantly simple ideas.

Perhaps the legend from Leonardo's life that inspires overachievers more than any other is his infamous sleep schedule. He reportedly slept no more than two hours a day, depending on the historical account. It wasn't that he only got a solid block at night from midnight to 2:00 am in the morning. It was that every four hours, he would take a 15-minute nap. He would plop down, immediately enter REM sleep, rise up again, and go back to inventing, political theorizing, or whatever it was he happened to be up to that day. He would then go for another four hours and then sleep for 15 minutes more. Leonardo continued with this cycle around the clock and got six 15-minute naps a day, totaling 90 minutes. He kept up this pattern continuously. Some theorized this eccentric sleep schedule allowed him to get so much work done in his life.

It's a tempting explanation to help us understand his enormous output. But doubts immediately come to mind. First of all, is it truth or urban myth? Second, is such a thing even possible in the human body, and if so, has anyone else done it? The first question is difficult to answer. The person who has done the most research on this aspect of Leonardo's life is Dr. Claudio Stampi, the Italian director and sole proprietor of the Chronobiology Research Institute, which conducts research on short naps in extreme conditions. According to Stampi, no credible source exists that describes Leonardo keeping up such sleeping patterns.

There is good reason to doubt that Da Vinci maintained this schedule. He lived before the invention of the light bulb; it would have been quite difficult to rouse oneself awake at 4 am with no illumination besides candlelight. Moreover, Da Vinci was known for becoming engrossed in his work and disregarding every other obligation. According to one account of his work on the Last Supper, he labored continuously from dawn until dusk and neglected food and drink. It is unlikely that he would remain so committed to a sleep schedule that required exact precision. Perhaps his sleep schedule is a myth that developed after his death to explain his eccentric approach to life.

But even if he did have the organizational ability, is such a sleep schedule possible in the human body? According to sleep research, such a schedule is actually possible. Practitioners call it polyphasic sleep. The general scientific principle is that the health benefits of sleep come from the REM cycle, which do not happen throughout an eight-hour slumber. It only occurs a couple of hours each night; the rest of the time the body lies in inefficient unconsciousness. If one can learn to fall into REM sleep, then they can save many hours in the process. Humans theoretically do not need eight hours of sleep for any biological regeneration. Giraffes weigh several hundred pounds but only need one and a half hours of sleep. If they can do it, why can't a human?

The legend of Leonardo's sleep schedule, whether real or a myth, lives on throughout popular culture. One of the best examples is a Seinfeld episode from Season 7 in which Kramer attempts to do the same. He keeps up the napping schedule for a few days. Eventually Kramer's attempt falls apart, with expected disastrous results.

Leaving aside Leonardo's sleep schedule, we will consider a final attribute of his life that explained his prodigious productivity. He took action. He took risks. Simply put, he understood that if one wants to accomplish things, he must do things. If one wants massive results they must take massive action. He did not substitute thinking for action. If one takes little action, it becomes easy to overestimate the value of results. One small failure or mistake can be blown out of proportion, causing emotional paralysis. But as Leonardo took more action, he felt less emotional effect from his results. He did not fall into a sad state if an experiment failed. He also did not rest on his laurels if he succeeded. Leonardo valued forward momentum, and he rarely lost his pace.

"Although nature commences with reason and ends in experience, it is necessary for us to do the opposite," he said. "That is, to commence with experience and from this to proceed to investigate the reason."

Experience never makes a mistake. Only judgment makes a mistake in promising itself results that are not caused by experiments. To this end, and to his credit, he never stopped experimenting.

CHAPTER SEVEN

GEORG PHILIPP TELEMANN (1681-1767)

Few composers write more than one or two symphonies in their lifetime. Beethoven spent a year on his shorter symphonies but more than six years on his 9th Symphony. The prodigy Mozart finished his last three symphonies (39, 40, and 41) in the span of a few weeks. His 25th Symphony took only two days.

However, none of these speed records match those of baroque composer Georg Philipp Telemann. Friends with both Johann Sebastian Bach and George Frideric Handel, he was the most prolific composer in history and considered to be a leading German composer at a time when some of the greatest classical composers in history lived. During his duties as court musician for Count Erdmann II of Promnitz in Poland he composed at least 200 overtures in a two-year period. Over his lifetime Telemann's oeuvre consists of more than 3,000 pieces, although "only" 800 survive to this day. His output was so high that it hurt his reputation a century after his death. Lexicographers dismissed him as a "polygraph," a *Vielschrieber* who valued quantity over quality.

Telemann was born in Magdeburg, Brandenburg [Germany] in 1681. He was surrounded by music from his birth due to his father's vocation. Telemann's father was not a musician – he was a Protestant minister – but in the 1600s Germany's churches were filled with music. Martin Luther's Reformation, begun in 1517, focused on a religious expression that could be experienced by the masses. Choral music replaced chanted liturgies. Church leaders made extensive use of the chorale as musical accompaniment to the church service. From these choral melodies much of traditional German baroque music grew. Organists elaborated on the chorale, either by adding interpolations between verses or composing whole sets of variations based on the original sets.

Unlike other classical composers, Georg received no formal music education during his childhood. Other than a few singing lessons and two weeks of organ instruction, he acquired the fundamentals of music through self-study. His exceptional ability soon led him away from the path of becoming a clergyman, which his family expected of him. He soon mastered the violin, flute, cither, and piano. Georg transcribed scores in order to learn composition. He pored over the works of Jean Baptiste Lully and Andre Campra. He then began to write his own music at the age of 10. Telemann composed pieces of church music and wrote most of his first opera "Sigismundus" by the age of 12. He learned other instruments such as the organ, oboe, shalm, and double bass. In an amazing demonstration of the variety of his capacity, while he developed musical prowess, he also acquired law instruction in Magdeburg, Zellerfeld and Hildesheim.

Telemann composed music against the wishes of his family. The work of a composer had not attained the level of respect it would after the 18th-century rise of classical music. His mother confiscated his instruments to discourage his career choice. It was to no avail. He threw himself into musical studies after leaving home for university. While he was a student in Leipzig University he founded the *Collegium Musicum*, an organization through which he gave public concerts, and wrote operatic works for the Leipzig Theatre. In 1703 he became musical director of the Leipzig Opera and was appointed organist at the Neue Church in 1704. He then accepted an appointment as chapelmaster (Kapellmeister) for the court of Count Erdmann II of Promnitz at Zary in 1705.

Telemann went on to hold important positions in numerous German courts before his posting as chapelmaster at the courts of Eisenach and Frankfurt. In 1721 he was appointed Hamburg's musical director for the city's five main churches. He visited Berlin numerous times, Paris in 1737, and other European centers of music throughout his life. He remained in Hamburg until his death in 1767. He was succeeded in his post at Hamburg by his godson, Carl Philipp Emanuel Bach, son of Johann Sebastian.

Through his travels and studies Telemann gained fluency in a number of musical genres. His style incorporated Italian, French, German, and Polish national styles, allowing him to remain at the forefront of musical innovation throughout his life. This melding of styles was dubbed the *style galant*. He was the first composer to adopt influences from the entire European continent and blur the lines between secular and sacred music, a critical influence on the evolution of German baroque music.

Telemann had a natural ability to compose. Handel once said of him that he could write a church piece of eight parts as simply as another would write a letter. His thousands of works include 1,000 orchestra suites, 600 overtures in the French style, 40 operas, 44 Passions, 12 complete cantata cycles for the liturgical year – which is more than 1,700 church cantatas – symphonies, sonatas, violin solos, duets, quartets, and piano and organ pieces. He wrote 45 liturgical passions, five oratorio passions, and seven sacred oratorios. He composed 15 motets, a Magnificat, and several Latin masses.

His unconventional background in music gave him advantages over properly trained musicians. Telemann was self-taught, giving him freedom from the more rigid German discipline of composition based on out-of-date musical writing techniques. Telemann wrote in his 1731 autobiography that he decided at an early stage to avoid complexities of traditional German music and write pieces that would appeal to mass audiences of varying levels of taste. Of church music, he said, "I not only endeavored to employ all instruments according to their individual qualities, but also with an intent for lightness, as I have almost always done in all of my other compositions."

Telemann's high productivity was also brought about by necessity. He wrote scores at moments of urgent need and had no assistance in creating or obtaining necessary texts or in composing and scoring his own works – unlike J.S. Bach, who had support from students and his family. But he believed that simple music aimed at the populace instead of court aristocrats served society better. So impassioned was Telemann in creating music for the masses that he wrote an ode to his simple style:

> For I am of the belief –
> A movement that contains sorcery in its lines
> I mean, when the page contains many difficult passages,
> almost always makes music a burden,
> whereby one often notices plenty of grimaces.
> I say furthermore; one who can be of use to many,
> does better than he who writes something only for the few;
> What is simply composed, now universally serves everyone;
> Therefore it will be best, that one remains with this [practice].

Telemann's 1721 appointment as Hamburg's musical director required all of his productive powers. Swain's *Historical Dictionary of Baroque Music* details his work responsibilities. He was required to compose two new cantatas for each Sunday, with one to be sung before the gospel reading and one after, as well as a new passion for

Lent, along with various occasional works for civic celebrations. He also directed the city's *collegium musicum*, a series of public concerts that became so popular that performances doubled from weekly to twice weekly. To add even more to his workload, Telemann became director of the Hamburg Gänsemarkt Opera in 1722, where he performed operas written by himself and composers Reinhard Keiser, and Handel.

Another factor of his productivity was creating a product that was in high enough demand to justify such a level of output. Telemann understood better than his contemporaries of the changes that the eighteenth century brought to European culture. Musicians need to appeal to a general populace of music lovers instead of only wealthy patrons. Buelow notes in *A History of Baroque Music* that his sacred music was crafted for average parishioners rather than any of Hamburg's social elite. Bach ignored this fact until Telemann involved him with his *collegium musicum* concerts in Leipzig. Handel also recognized this change and turned his attention from aristocratic opera audiences to find wider acceptance with his sacred and secular oratorios.

As if his compositional output weren't high enough, Telemann had interests beyond music. He published poetry, anthologized between 1723 and 1738. As a publisher, he released 43 collections of his own music and engraved the plates himself. These works are considered encyclopedic surveys of genres and techniques of his own time, particularly the *Essercizii Musici* (1739), *Musique de Table* (1733), and *Der getreue Music-Meister* (1728). By the 1740s he drifted into retirement, but Joseph Swain notes that his productivity hardly slowed. Telemann still wrote a passion for Hamburg every year until his death. He found a new burst of energy to compose late in life when new sacred poetry became popular.

His publishing activities were almost as important for this history of music as his music itself. Telemann pursued exclusive publication rights, setting an early precedent for regarding music as the intellectual property of the composer. This fact is obvious in the age of RIAA lawsuits, but in the early 18th century music was generally considered to be property of the patron, much like newspaper articles remain the property of the publisher, not the journalist. A similar attitude informed his public concerts. Telemann frequently performed music originally composed for ceremonies attended by a few members of the upper class. He earned major profits on his works that were published to the masses for sale.

Beyond his work habits and music talent, there is another explanation for Telemann's ability to create so much music. His likeable personality and sense of humor kept him in the good graces of his patrons, fans, and critics alike. He was admired and envied, rather than resented for earning top court and church positions. Telemann possessed enough self-confidence to maneuver in elite political circles. He had the courage to challenge superiors when they interfered with his plans to perform in opera houses or publish his own works. Because of his output, Telemann's salaried income at Hamburg was approximately three times what Bach earned at Leipzig.

Critics have maligned Telemann for his high level of output. Much like literary critics of Isaac Asimov in the 20th century, they consider Telemann to have a lunch-pail approach to music, more craftsman than artist, whose compositions lacked depth and profundity because of the little time his spent editing or redrafting his scores. Most critics agree that he had natural ability and could write charming music on a whim. But whether this charming music reached the levels of genius of Mozart, Bach, or Haydn are more contested.

Contemporary classical music lovers are still torn over his legacy. In 1981 the New York Times wrote an article on a production of Telemann's "Canary Cantata." It notes that while the baroque composer was considered the wonder of his age and played "many a fine and joyous sound," he was above all a craftsman, and more of a composer of the early classical period than Bach and Handel. "Telemann was a very practical pension," said Sally Sanford, soprano in the ensemble. "He really mastered all the cliches of his style." His music was described as having an easy, slick sound. "The sacred and secular works are the same," said harpsichordist Frederick Renz. "Telemann never gets too profound. The Canary Cantata is about as heavy as he gets."

His music did have an easy style, but it was also influenced by multiple sources. Music scholars note the continent-wide musical influences found in his scores, whether German, Italian, French, English, or Polish. They are like a museum that showcases the different European genres of the early 18th century. His promiscuous approach to cultural influences allowed him to be creative yet productive. In his biography he talks of conducting music in the Polish style.

I had an opportunity in upper Silesia as well as in Cracow of getting to know Polish music in all its barbaric beauty. One would hardly believe what wonderfully bright ideas such pipers and fiddlers are apt to get when they improvise, ideas that would suffice for an entire lifetime. There is in this music a great deal of merit provided it is treated right. I have myself written in this manner several large concertos and trios that I clad in Italian clothes with alternating Adagio and Allegrio.

Arguments over the most productive musician in history typically fall into a debate between Mozart and Telemann. Champions of Wolfgang argued that he died at such a young age that if his life is analyzed by his rate of musical output rather then total tally, then he beats Telemann. Mozart is clearly the more famous of the two musicians. He has the most recordings, annual music festivals, and hours dedicated to him on public radio stations across the United States. Well-to-do parents even believe that playing Mozart to their unborn children will increase their intelligence.

But while Mozart might be considered the greater musical genius, it is Telemann who is the most productive. His legacy was his music. He unashamedly made it simple and accessible to the populace, producing as much as possible. When Telemann died in his home in 1767, a Hamburg newspaper printed that "his name is his eulogy."

CHAPTER EIGHT

RICHARD FRANCIS BURTON (1821-1890)

In the throes of a harsh Arabian summer, Al-Haj Abdullah traveled along the dusty road to Mecca to perform his Islamic pilgrimage, thankful he rode on camelback and was not shuffling along on foot like a pack animal, like his two servants. He traveled along with a caravan during July of 1853 and kept friendly, if distant, relations with the other men in his company. They were nevertheless interested in his exotic background. He had already traveled a considerable distance to arrive this far. Al-Haj Abdullah was an Indian-born Afghani, educated at Rangoon as an Islamic scholar. To get this far he would have had to travel through Central Asia, take a ship across the Black Sea to Constantinople, then journey south to Egypt, and finally to the Arabian Peninsula. Such a man must have had incredible resolve and wisdom to pass through and survive so many foreign lands and cultures.

They had no idea. After all, Al-Haj Abdullah was not the man he claimed to be. The scholar's previous identity was an Islamic mystic from Iran. He had presented himself as a Persian nobleman before swapping out his fluent Persian with accented Arabic. But his true identity was also not that of an Islamic mystic. The deepest layer of his matryoshka doll of personalities – and the real one – was that of Richard Francis Burton, a British army officer, master linguist, expert in arms, and one of the top world travelers of the nineteenth century.

Richard Francis Burton was a British consul, Orientalist, explorer, and linguist, best known for translating the *Arabian Nights* and the *Kama Sutra* into English. He was the most educated explorer of the Victorian age. He discovered the source of the Nile with his expedition partner, John Hanning Speke, notable particularly because it was typically only men of rough disposition who set out to discover foreign lands. The landed gentry were uninterested in international travel, unless it was in the comfort of a steamship to go administer a colony for the sake of the Crown or as a military officer deployed to extend the global landholdings of the British Empire.

Burton was also an accomplished author and published nearly 50 books, ranging from such topics as linguistics, ethnology, poetry, geography, fencing, and travel narratives, the history of the sword, and grammars of Amazonian tribes. He spoke 29 languages, including Greek, Arabic, Persian, Icelandic, Turkish, Swahili, Hindi, and a host of other European, Asian, and African tongues.

Burton's productivity did not come from maintaining strict habits like Benjamin Franklin or Isaac Asimov. Rather, he managed to keep perpetually busy and take advantage of any opportunity that came to him, even if the "opportunity" was a useless job or a demotion. Burton wrote dozens of books during times when his diplomatic appointment to an unimportant post in an African or South American backwater required little work. He used the time to discover unknown tribes, go incognito into the Middle East, or hike the extent of the Andes Mountains.

Richard Francis Burton was born in 1821 to a wealthy family of influence from Devon. His father Joseph Burton was lieutenant-colonel of the 36th Regiment, inspiring his son's interest in military affairs and travel. Burton was also believed, mostly by his numerous critics, to be partially of Romany descent. They "saw gypsy written in his peculiar eyes as in his character, wild and resentful, essentially vagabond, intolerant of convention and restrain." Whatever his lineage, Burton committed enough audacious acts in his childhood to warrant such an accusation.

His family traveled frequently in his youth. He spent his childhood in France and Italy, where he demonstrated an early propensity for foreign language and imitating foreign customs so well as to be mistaken for a local. He obtained rapid fluency in the vernacular languages. He began his education in France under a series of tutors and then his formal education in 1829 at a prep school in Surrey. Burton soon spoke French and Italian with ease and translated Latin verse. His live-wire personality also presented itself early in his life. As a youth he ran a fencing foil through the back of his brother's mouth. He bashed his violin over his music master's head. Such an untrammeled childhood did not prepare him for the stiff, formal university education that came in his eighteenth year.

Burton made use of his foreign travels to learn about new skills and cultures, knowledge that made him the prolific explorer and author of his later years. He enlisted in the East India Company in 1842 when the first Afghan War was still unfinished. He joined the Sindh survey in 1843, which afforded him permission to wander freely around the Muslim portions of India, the least-explored land in the British colony, and learn the main languages of the region. He lived for weeks among private teachers and learned native customs to the point of disappearing among the local population. English officers rarely interacted with the natives of British-occupied India beyond their servants, bureaucrats, merchants, translators, or anyone else in their direct employ. Thus Burton was thought odd by the men with whom he served. At this time he qualified in four more languages – Marathi, Sindhi, Punjabi, and Persian – while also studying Pashtu, Sanskrit, and Arabic.

During his surveying operation of the Sindh, Burton crafted an alter ego. He donned traditional Muslim dress and introduced himself as "Mirza Abdullah" to gain closer access to the Indian Islamic community. He became conversant in the Qur'an from his knowledge of Arabic and in Sufi philosophy from his knowledge of Persian. Keeping up his ruse would not be a problem if conversation with his "brethren" turned to religion. He practiced Islamic religious precepts such as the customary five daily prayers to further penetrate theological circles. He was so adept in his new identity that many British soldiers did not recognize him.

In 1849 Burton's health diminished because of his work in the sandy deserts of Sindh, which brought on ophthalmia. He returned to Europe disappointed in this forced convalescence but managed to bring back with him a substantial collection of oriental manuscripts and curios. These formed the basis of five books about India that he published in the next three years. He spent a year writing his first book, *Goa and the Blue Mountains*, an in-depth guide to the region in India. His other works were the two-volume *Sind, or the Unhappy Valley*; *Sind, and the Races that Inhabit the Valley of the Indus*; *Falconry in the Valley of the Indus*, and *A Complete System of Bayonet Exercises*. These works came to the attention of other parties in Britain, who thought his abilities could be better used for exploration than for military intelligence. The Royal Geographical Society and the British East India Company requested that he lead teams through the Middle East and India. The army permitted him an indeterminate leave of absence to explore for these two organizations at their request.

Burton knew how to create opportunities for himself. During his four years in England he dreamed of conducting the pilgrimage to Mecca in disguise, an idea that first came to him while in India among the Muslims of Sind. He set out with a group of Muslims from Egypt and took every precaution to assimilate. Burton did not only act as an Arab – he *became* an Arab, adopting the culture and customs of the people, even becoming circumcised to reduce his risk of being discovered as an imposter. The group continued onward to Mecca, where Burton donned the *ihram*, a distinctive garb of white unsewn cloth worn by a male pilgrim. Over the next five days he joined a procession of thousands who converged on Mecca and performed the steps of the pilgrimage.

Ultimately, he succeeded in his journey, receiving the honor of referring to himself as "hajji" and permission to wear the green turban of a Muslim who had completed the pilgrimage. Burton published his account *A Personal Narrative of a Pilgrimage to Al-Medinah and Meccah* in 1855. The British public received it to great acclaim for its vivid descriptions, insight into Arab manners, keen observations, dry humor, and uncouth language.

Burton parlayed this success into another mission. He set out for a more dangerous adventure without bothering to recuperate in England. In 1854 Burton returned to Cairo from Mecca and sailed to India to rejoin his regiment. He then requested permission to explore the interior of Somalia. The colonial administrators approved his request – who better to travel through the unknown and hostile tribal country of savagery and cannibalism? – and transferred him to Aden on the Persian Gulf. This expedition was supported by the Royal Geographic Society in order to discover large lakes in the African interior that Arab nomads had claimed to have seen. He was to be accompanied by Lieutenant John Speke but undertook the first part of the expedition alone, traveling to the forbidden city of Harar in East Africa. The Somali capital, located in present-day Ethiopia, was a city which no European had ever entered. Burton characteristically overcame this challenge by traveling in disguise and reassumed the identity of Arab merchant Haji Mirza Abdullah.

Burton reconvened with Speke and two other officers. Shortly after, the group set out from the port of Berberah to the African interior. The group had hardly begun their journey when they were attacked by a Somali raiding party. A hailstorm of spears fell upon them. The enemy swarmed in like hornets with shouts and battle cries intended to terrify. Lieutenant Stroyan of the party was killed, while Lieutenant Speke was suffered eleven wounds. Burton barely escaped with his life after he had a javelin thrust through his jaws; it passed completely through both cheeks, where it remained during the party's escape. It knocked out four teeth and transfixed his palate. The cheek-to-cheek wound gave him a permanent but distinctive scar that appeared in all his famous portraits and photographs.

Despite the party's heroic escape from the raiding party, the expedition was seen as a failure. British authorities launched a two-year investigation to determine the extent of Burton's blame and whether his intrepid behavior was in fact utter recklessness. They eventually cleared him of these charges, an ordeal that he detailed in his 1856 book *First Footsteps in East Africa*. The book was a bestseller and received positive reviews for its erudition, observation, and humor. Burton was always able to turn an expedition, even a failed expedition, into a book. No opportunity was lost for productive output, even if the original mission did not succeed.

In 1856 the Royal Geographic Society commissioned him again to search for the source of the Nile. The upper reaches of the Nile had been a mystery to the ancient Greeks and Romans ever since Herodotus' description of the river in his *Histories*. Every expedition to discover its source had ended in failure. No European expedition had ever attempted to reach the Nile's source, and the most recent information on its location came from Ptolemy's geographical works 2,000 years earlier. In 1857 Burton rejoined Speke to lead an expedition into Central Africa to succeed where others had failed by penetrating past the Ethiopian highlands and into South Sudan. Burton used a route never taken before, traveling overland from Kenya through modern-day Tanzania. He used reports from German missionaries, who brought back native stories of the existence of the lake.

Difficulties plagued the expedition from the beginning, including burglary and bouts of disease that left Speke temporarily blind. Their servants were untrustworthy. Local tribes opposed them. But after months of journeying through thick jungle, word spread through the expedition that a massive lake had been spotted. On February 14, 1858, they reached Lake Tanganyika, the largest of the Central Africa Lakes. It was clear, however, that its hydrological characteristics and location ruled it out as the source of the Nile.

The two returned to England separately, but Speke arrived first due to Burton's illness and period of convalescence in Aden. Speke used this head start to obtain funding from the Royal Society for a second expedition to Central Africa. Burton also applied for funding and was accepted but could not commit to a start date. The division between the two explorers was heightened by their contrasting cultural background – Speke was the quintessential British aristocrat and imperialist, Burton the open-minded *tramp royale*. Their rivalry continued until Speke's death in 1864.

Burton then switched careers. Two months after his marriage to Isabel Arundell, a 19-year-old aristocrat, Burton entered the Foreign Service as consul at Fernando Po, an island 20 miles off the west coast of Africa in modern-day Equatorial Guinea. It was the beginning of the first of many long periods of separation. Isabel could not accompany him due to the hostile climate and foreign diseases of Africa that threatened the health of visiting Europeans. Burton traveled outside his jurisdiction and into the African interior when not occupied with diplomatic duties, which was quite often, as his post was in an unimportant part of the Commonwealth. On one such trip he became the first European to climb the Cameroon Mountains and ascended the Congo River as far as the Yellala Falls. Burton even visited the French settlement of Gaboon in order to capture a gorilla.

In 1865 he was transferred to the consulship of Santos, Brazil, where Isabel joined him. Here he visited gold and diamond mines of inland Brazil and returned to the coast by a solo 1,500-mile voyage down the São Francisco River. He also crossed the Andes to see Peru, Chile, and the Strait of Magellan. Another expedition took him to the killing fields of the bloody Paraguayan War. He left São Paulo and arrived at Montevideo in June 1868, then crossed into Buenos Aires after 10 days. He then traveled upstream to Humaitá, in Paraguay, the scene of the worst fighting in the war. This was an unproductive period by Burton's standards, but voluminous by anyone else's – he wrote two books during this diplomatic posting: *Explorations of the Highlands of the Brazil* (1869) and *Letters from the Battlefields of Paraguay* (1870).

The Foreign Service appointed him consul in Damascus four years later – his desired posting when he first joined the consulship. Isabel joined him shortly after, and the couple enjoyed life in Syria, the cultural and cosmopolitan center of the Middle East in the mid-nineteenth century. Burton conducted archeological excavations with the famed scientists Charles Tyrwhitt-Drake and Edward Henry Palmer. The group unearthed the first-known Hittite antiquities.

The 51-year-old's pace of exploration slowed down at this point in his life. He was transferred to Europe and remained at the same diplomatic post until his death. It required little work of him and the Foreign Office permitted him to travel and write. Burton and Isabel explored the Roman ruins and prehistoric castellieri of Istria. They visited the Etruscan antiquities of Bologna. In 1876 the two traveled to India and revisited his old haunts of Goa and Sindh.

From the 1880s onward Burton realized he was no longer able to embark on the same ambitious journeys. He committed himself to recording his travels and publishing his translations of Arabic and Persian poetry. Over the years Burton had accumulated a mountain of manuscripts in dozens of languages. At this time he published his most famous translations, in particular the 10-volume project on Luís Vaz de Camões, the sixteenth-century Portuguese poet considered to be the greatest writer in his language. The epic poems are a romantic take on the Age of Discovery in the Indian Ocean. It is easy to imagine Burton seeing his own career in the poetic verse, and the poet as a brother in travel. He preserved the meter, rhetorical style, and archaic language with great precision. Burton's second great work was *The Book of the Sword*, a history of the weapon and its use in all kingdoms and nations, from the Neolithic Age to the modern era.

He is best known for his translations of the *Kama Sutra*, *The Arabian Nights* and *The Perfumed Garden of the Shaykh Nefzawi*. His 10-volume translation of the *Arabian Nights* in particular flew off the shelves of British bookstores. It earned the author a profit of £10,000, worth nearly £1 million ($1.8 million) today. Burton finished these projects in the final years of his life. He died in 1891 at the age of 70.

Today Richard Francis Burton is not a household name when compared to explorers like Ferdinand Magellan and Captain Cook, or modern explorers like Stanley and Livingstone. This is despite his arguably superior intellect, bravery, and productivity. He was, however, well known in literary circles. Many of his books are more famous than the man himself. Burton's seemingly insatiable appetites are evident through all of his writing, particularly in the *Kama Sutra*, which contains detailed images of sexual positions. His obsession was widely known, and led to considerable censure of Burton's work.

But he has many lessons to impart to us today about productivity. Burton took advantage of every situation in his life. If the Royal Society permitted him to travel to the headwaters of the Nile, he jumped in with reckless abandon. But if a diplomatic posting gave him little to do, he used the time to write a book, travel to unexplored lands, or take a 2,000-mile solo kayaking trip.

Above all, he did so out of a spirit of adventure. He wrote in his journal during an expedition to Zanzibar in 1856:"Of the gladdest moments in human life, methinks is the departure upon a distant journey to unknown lands. Shaking off with one mighty effort the fetters of habit, the leaden weight of Routine, the cloak of many Cares and the Slavery of Home, man feels once more happy. The blood flows with the fast circulation of childhood….afresh dawns the morn of life…"

CHAPTER NINE

ISAAC ASIMOV (1920-1992)

For decades the middle-aged man with a shock of gray hair and horn-rimmed glasses that looked like they belonged in a NASA control room pounded furiously away at his typewriter. He sat in the attic of his house, encircled by bookcases built low because of the sloping ceilings. Over 1,000 volumes of history, science, literature, and everything else filled the shelves. Well over 100 of the books on these shelves were written by him, and these were only one-fourth of the books that he would write over his lifetime.

Isaac Asimov, the late doyen of science fiction, had a literary output that frightened all but the most prolific novelists. Over his lifetime he wrote or edited more than 500 books and hundreds of short stories and essays, and fired off 90,000 letters and postcards to fans around the world. Asimov's books were published in nine of the 10 major categories of the Dewey Decimal System. His most famous work is the *Foundation Series*, but he is also known for his prescient descriptions of artificial intelligence and creating the Three Laws of Robotics.

For a writer to produce an output that voluminous, he would need to write one book every two weeks for 25 years. Since each of his books were approximately 70,000 words, that works out to roughly 5,000 words a day, ready for publication. Almost any writer will tell you that the first go-around is *not* ready for publication, suggesting Asimov's total work count was much higher. He ran everything through the typewriter at least twice.

Asimov's Gatling-style approach to writing took years to cultivate, but it began after the release of his first novel. His first published work was a 1938 short story "Marooned Off Vesta," a 6,400-word piece he wrote when he was 18. His first book appeared 12 years later, *Pebble in the Sky*. The same year he released the landmark story collection *I Robot*. The next year saw the release of *Foundation*, the first book in his seven-part series that explored the fall of a galactic empire and a statistical method of predicting the future known as "psychohistory." From this point on he began to crank out science fiction at an even faster pace, along with many other genres of books. He wrote essays, instruction books, poetry, history, collections of dirty limericks, and even an introduction to the slide rule. With his long hours at work, Asimov could sometimes finish entire books in a few days.

In many ways, Asimov was the anti-writer. The image of a novelist sitting at a typewriter, straining to produce each word and tearing up a manuscript if it is not perfect haunts the imaginations of many first-time writers. For this reason there are many self-proclaimed "writers" who never write. They claim the title as their profession but never put out a word due to paralysis by analysis. *Writer's block*, they say.

Too many people believe that the key to excellent writing is to meditate at one's keyboard and only spoon out tiny serving of words whenever the muse whispers in their ear. Then before moving forward must come the edit and re-edit of each sentence until it is perfect. Such a process seems appropriate for creating a literary work of art – like a painter at a canvas dabbing away with microscopic brushstrokes – but it is not how Asimov did his craft.

How did he do it? It wasn't by a slow, contemplative process. Asimov wrote in a fast, straightforward style and attacked the page in his typewriter, believing that output was far better than deeply nuanced dithering. The New York Times profiled Asimov in 1969 to understand the secret of his prodigious output. At that point in his career he had already written 10 million words, totaling over 100 books. A reporter followed him for a day and broke down his daily routine, step-by-step.

Asimov worked seven days a week. He woke up at 6 am, breakfasted, and went to the post office at 8 am sharp. He was a morning caller, meaning that he collected his own mail rather than wait for delivery. Part of the reason was to eliminate junk mail at its source. A larger part of it was to take an early dose of positive motivation. His mail typically included fan letters, royalty checks, an invitation to write for a science fiction anthology, or a publisher's contract. He could visibly witness the fruit of his labor, motivating him to go back to his attic and pound at his typewriter once again.

He started writing between 9:30 and 10 am, typing over 90 words a minute until 5 o'clock. Asimov took only small breaks, rarely more than a small lunch and a coffee break. His office had a window with a view of a willow tree in his yard, but he rarely looked at it. Nor did he cut the grass in his lawn. That would take away from writing time.

Asimov then stopped for dinner. Sometimes he spent time with his wife and two teenage children. They would watch TV or read together. Asimov preferred reading magazines, mysteries, or science fiction. They could even drag him out of the house on occasion. But usually he went back to work after dinner and kept writing until 10 pm. He then finished the day the way he started it by taking outgoing mail to a box in front of a nearby junior high school. When somnolence took over, Asimov slept, probably drafting an outline for the next part of the book in his sleep.

Asimov explained in "In Memory Yet Green," the first volume of his 1979 autobiography, how he became a tireless writer. His Jewish Russian father owned a number of candy stores in Brooklyn that were open from 6 am to 1 am each day in order to cater to the hours of its urban clientele. The younger Asimov assisted his father at different intervals until he was 27. He awoke at 6 to deliver the morning newspapers, went to school, then rushed home to help out in the store each afternoon. If he were late, his father would call him a "folyack," a Yiddish word for slacker. The habit of early rising became a permanent habit.

This lunch pail approach to writing, producing words on the paper even if the muse did not visit him and scoffing at the idea of "writer's block," (store owners like his father never shut the doors due to "shop keeper's block") influenced his style more than anything else. As a result, no one publisher could keep up with Asimov's output. He was like an amorous polygamist that required a harem of wives and concubines to keep him satisfied. Both Doubleday and Houghton Mifflin published nearly everything he gave to them, and they only handled 60 percent of his work. The rest was covered by small presses, science fiction magazines, and author anthologies.

His productivity also came from a commitment to writing that bordered on workaholism. Rarely could Asimov's wife Gertrude drag him away from the house for a vacation. She recalled that in the mid-1960s she made him give in. They went to Cape Ann in New York. Upon arrival, the college student personnel of the hotel, who were arranging a parody of Cole Porter's "Kiss Me Kate" asked Asimov to help with lyrics. He spent seven days at the typewriter working on the manuscript, never going outside. Asimov didn't even see the show. (One guest reported that while the music was subpar, the lyrics were excellent.)

In one twist of irony, the reason that the science fiction writer – who spent thousands of pages contemplating the future of rocketry and deep space exploration – was able to write is because he rarely traveled due to his fear of flying. He was a fierce rationalist who had an irrational fear of heights. This limited the range of his travels, keeping him close to his home and his home office.

But it was not only Asimov's number of work hours that enabled him to produce so much content. He preferred a completely unembellished writing style. His characters were simple and the plot functional. The dialogue was so straightforward that it approached the telegraphic minimum of language. There is little literary criticism on Asimov despite his widespread popularity and influence as a writer. This is because Asimov stated so clearly to the reader what is happening in the story and why it is happening. Characters do not speak so much as exposit. There is very little for critics to interpret when characters do the work for them.

In 1980, science fiction scholar James Gunn, wrote of *I, Robot* the following.

> Except for two stories—"Liar!" and "Evidence"—they are not stories in which character plays a significant part. Virtually all plot develops in conversation with little if any action. Nor is there a great deal of local color or description of any kind. The dialogue is, at best, functional and the style is, at best, transparent.... The robot stories and, as a matter of fact, almost all Asimov fiction, play themselves on a relatively bare stage.

Asimov was never offended by such criticism. To the contrary, he welcomed it. He followed in the writing tradition of authors such as Ernest Hemingway, who favored short sentences, direct speech, strong verbs, and powerful prose. He believed that flowery language, useless adverbs, and nonsensical metaphors would only clutter up his writing and make it more of a chore for the reader. Here's how he described his own approach to writing.

I made up my mind long ago to follow one cardinal rule in all my writing—to be clear. I have given up all thought of writing poetically or symbolically or experimentally, or in any of the other modes that might (if I were good enough) get me a Pulitzer Prize. I would write merely clearly and in this way establish a warm relationship between myself and my readers, and the professional critics—well, they can do whatever they wish.

Despite his plain writing style and lukewarm relationship with literary scholars, Asimov's influence spans decades. A generation of Apollo Program-age scientists were influenced by his writing, raised on his belief that there is nothing we cannot master. His simple style encouraged readers to see the world as comprehensible. His star has only shone brighter in the years since his death in 1992. His utopian vision of a future driven by progress stands in optimistic contrast to the modern cyberpunk genres that describe dystopias, evil multinational corporations, outlaws, and nihilism. And his honest, humorous, unpretentious style shines through it all.

PART III

STATESMEN

CHAPTER TEN

JULIUS CAESAR (100-44 BC)

Who is the greatest military leader in history? How can that even be determined? Can generals who lived 2,000 years ago and conquered empires by the edges of spears and military units offer wisdom to 21st century generals that conquer by pilotless drones, aircraft carriers, and Hellfire missiles?

Military historian Barry Strauss set out to answer this question of history's greatest general in his 2013 book "Master of Command: Alexander, Hannibal, Caesar, and the Genius of Leadership." He compared the qualities of the these generals according to three levels of criteria. First, they marshaled and directed armies; second, they used them for optimal strategic effect; third, they transformed these military victories into political power.

According to this schema, Hannibal was the most brilliant battlefield tactician. His triumph at Cannae, in which he achieved double encirclement by a smaller army against a larger enemy, was such a stroke of battlefield genius that it could only be repeated

1,000 years later by Khalid ibn al-Walid. Alexander was the greatest mobilizer of manpower and mobilization. He could harness unlimited money and soldiers by converting his cult of celebrity into a devoted fighting force. But it is Julius Caesar who is the greatest general. He alone transferred his victories into long-term strategic success. His victories laid the foundations of Roman power. For these reasons he was the patron saint of statesmen.

Julius Caesar earned his reputation by winning nearly all his battles. He personified the height of military and political power. His surname, Caesar, which was common in his lifetime and had no special meaning, became posthumously synonymous with "king" and "emperor" in multiple languages ("Kaiser" in German, "Czar" in Russian, "Qaysar" in Arabic, and "Sezer" in Turkish). His conquests changed not only Roman civilization, but also the political and military history of Western civilization.

Arnold Toynbee argues that by liquidating the scandalous and bankrupt rule of the Roman nobility, Caesar gave the Roman state—and with it the Greco-Roman civilization—a reprieve that lasted more than 600 years in the East and 400 years in the West. He extended the Roman Empire's domains as far north as Britain and as far south as Egypt. Caesar swapped out the Roman oligarchy for an autocracy. It could never afterward be abolished. If he had not done this when he did, Rome and the Greco-Roman world might have succumbed to barbarian invasions in the West and the Parthian Empire in the East. Unlike Hannibal, his political acumen matched his military ability. Caesar successfully transmuted his battlefield victories into political expansion and a permanent government that lasted for centuries after his death.

He was capable of such a high level of achievement because of his abilities. Toynbee notes that although Caesar was not personable, he won his soldiers' devotion with military victories brought about by his tactical brilliance. He won politicians' devotion due to his ability in administration, generalship, and propaganda.

Despite his successes on the battlefield, Caesar did not begin his career in the military. It began late and was as much a product of his ambition as his allegiance to Rome. He first studied to be a lawyer. Caesar gained a reputation as a talented prosecutor, using his oratorical abilities to bring corrupt government officials to justice. The position required travel, a dangerous prospect during his trips to the fringes of the Republic. In one such journey, Caesar was kidnapped by pirates as he crossed the Aegean Sea. When his captors demanded a ransom of 20 talents of silver, he demanded that it be raised to 50 in keeping with his social stature. In perhaps one of the most memorable stories of revenge in history, he also promised the pirates that upon his release, he would crucify them personally. They thought he was jesting. When the ransom was paid, he raised a fleet, pursued and captured the pirates, and imprisoned them. They died by his promised means of execution.

His political career turned to military affairs when in 69 BC, he became a tribune and quaestor in Spain. Caesar later experienced an existential crisis when the 30-something statesman looked upon a statue of Alexander the Great. He realized that the Macedonian general had accomplished his extraordinary conquests before reaching Caesar's age. Alexander had never lost a battle in his remarkable career and conquered much of the ancient world while Caesar was a mere administrator in a backwater Roman province who had frittered away his youth. Plutarch recounts this scene as follows: "It is matter for sorrow that while Alexander, at my age, was already king of so many peoples, I have as yet achieved no brilliant success."

Caesar's focus sharpened from this new sense of purpose. This crisis of self motivated him to rise through the ranks of the Roman military. He soon gained the rank of proconsul and earned command of a major military expedition in the Gallic Wars, an eight-year war against Gallic tribes, begun in 58 BC. He went into the Gallic Wars primarily as a means of self-validation in order to join the pantheon of the greatest generals in history. The more practical purpose for fighting the war was to boost Caesar's military career and retire his massive debts.

He contended with fierce tribesmen in modern-day France and Belgium. In 56 BC, Roman messengers went to the Gallic tribes to demand grain and provisions for their troops. The messengers were seized by the Veneti, a coastal maritime people living in modern-day Brittany. They promised the messengers' release in exchange for their own hostages. Caesar was in little mood to have his soldiers used as bargaining chips. He stormed their strongholds by raising siege works in order to enter their defenses. The Veneti fled in their trading vessels, which were sail-driven and lacked oars. Caesar's legate Junius Brutus was given command of the Roman naval fleet. In a decisive battle he destroyed the Veneti fleet in Quiberon Bay. The Romans used long billhooks to strike at the enemy's halyards – the rope used for raising and lowering sails – as they swept past, which caused the mainsails to drop to the deck. The Veneti ships were left stranded. The Romans were able to board, and the entire Veneti fleet surrendered. Caesar made an example out of their treachery against the Republic to other Gallic tribes. Everyone on the governing council was beheaded. The rest were sold into slavery.

Caesar's reputation as a competent battle commander did not go unnoticed by the Imperial Senate. In addition to crafting his own military victories, Caesar was frequently called to difficult battles to assist Roman generals unsuccessful at quelling rebellions. The Gauls revolted again in 54 BC, led by the Eburones under Ambiorix. The Gauls won a major victory at Atuatuca Tugrorum (modern Tongeren in Belgium) wiping out 15 Roman cohorts. Caesar arrived at the battle scene to stave off further Roman losses. He, in turn, destroyed the Eburones in a punitive campaign. In 53 BC Vercingetorix, chief of the Arverni tribe, fought a scorched earth campaign to deprive the Roman army of its supplies, prompting Caesar to return from Italy and lead a counterattack. He captured the town of Avaricum but failed to do so at Georgiva. Caesar then besieged Vercingetorix at Alesia and crushed his supply lines. He beat off a huge Gallic relief force, which ran out of food and had to disperse. With this decisive victory, the Gallic Wars had finally come to an end. Caesar had established himself as Rome's most effective and powerful military commander.

In addition to his command abilities, Caesar was able to acquire power due to his oratorical talent. Caesar was a masterly public speaker in an age in which he was in competition with Cicero. Toynbee notes that all of Caesar's speeches and writings, both those lost and still in existence, served political purposes. He even used his oration at his wife's funeral for political propaganda. His accounts of his wars are contrived to make the unsuspecting reader see Caesar's acts in the light that he chose. The accounts were written in the form of factual reports that looked impersonal, yet every recorded fact was carefully selected and presented. Despite their political purposes, his speeches are great literature. A reader looking beyond their prosaic purpose can appreciate them as works of art.

He also acquired power by his boundless intellectual and physical energy. Caesar could lead an army into battle and at the same time write a historical account of the battle itself. He prepared his books on the Gallic War – *Commentarii de Bello Gallico* – for publication in 51 BC while mopping up rebellions at the end of the war. He wrote his books on the civil war and his *Anticato* in the hectic years between 49 and 44 BC while simultaneously leading a military campaign. His physical energy was of the same level. In the winter of 57–56 BC he found time to visit his third province, Illyria, as well as Cisalpine Gaul. In the interval between his campaigns of 55-54 BC, he administered in Cisalpine Gaul and went to Illyria to settle accounts with the tribe of Pirustae in what is now Albania. In 49 BC he marched within a single campaigning season during the Great Roman Civil War from the Rubicon in northeastern Italy to Brundisium in southern Italy and from Brundisium to northern

Spain. At Alexandria, the 53-year-old Caesar saved himself from sudden death when Egyptians sailed up against his boat from all directions. He was forced to throw himself into the sea and swim, only just managing to escape.

Plutarch claims that Caesar could dictate letters on horseback and keep two scribes busy at once. Caesar's friend Gaius Oppius claimed that even two scribes were not enough for him. Pliny the Elder says that he dictated four letters at once, even up to seven during particularly busy periods. When Caesar traveled in a litter he kept a scribe beside him at all times. By these means he was able to write his detailed formal reports to the Senate, narrative accounts of battles, and his *Commentaries*, published in a seven-volume set in 46 BC. Throughout his reign he used dictation to establish a massive network of correspondence with friends and allies across the Empire.

Caesar endured the hardships of a political and military career despite a poor diet and disregard for his health. Once while on a journey he and his friends were driven into a poor man's hut by a storm. There was only one room. He said to his friends that honors must be yielded to the strongest but necessities to the weakest. He bade his subordinate Oppius to sleep in the hut while he and the rest of his company slept on the porch.

With all these productive powers at his disposal, Caesar, age 51, turned his capacities to taking control of the Roman Republic. It was an opportune time to strike. The end of the Gallic War meant the end of the First Triumvirate, an uneasy political alliance between three powerful Roman politicians, Marcus Licinius Crassus, Pompey the Great, and Caesar himself. Crassus had died in battle, and Pompey, the leader of the Senate, had aligned himself with Caesar's opponents. Pompey ordered Caesar to return to Rome in 50 BC due to the expiration of his term as governor. Caesar was concerned that he would be prosecuted if he lacked magisterial immunity.

In the most famous move of his career, which spawned a cliché of committing an irreversible action, Caesar crossed the Rubicon River with a legion, consisting of five thousand soldiers. As he stood on the banks of the river, he quoted the Athenian Menander with the Greek phrase, "The die is cast." This signaled the beginning of Caesar's Civil War, 49-45 BC. Pompey and the Senate escaped south as Caesar was declared dictator, despite his enemies having more troops.

Caesar chased Pompey across Europe, all the way to Egypt. Pompey met his end there; he was assassinated by counselors to King Ptolemy XIII. Caesar's final military victories were against Pharnaces II, a client king of Pompey's, then Pompey's sons in Spain, and finally Pompey's remaining senatorial supporters in Africa. These victories were executed swiftly and took only a few months. Caesar was given a decade-long appointment as dictator.

Gaius Julius Caesar was declared *Dictator perpetuo* (dictator in perpetuity) in 45 BC. He used this enormous political capital to tie up military loose ends left dangling on the periphery of the empire and enact political reform. Caesar centralized the government in order to curb armed resistance in the provinces, reduce corruption, and homogenize the empire, from Rome to the peripheries. New legislation encompassed everything, from debt reform and term limits for governors to grain purchases. He replaced the Roman lunar calendar with a solar calendar, known as the Julian calendar. Carthage and Corinth were rebuilt. The Senate named him censor for life and Father of the Fatherland.

He did not shy away from his subjects' tendency to engage in emperor worship. Minted coins bore Caesar's image. Statues were erected in the Senate of him sitting upon a golden chair. When he returned to Rome after his final military victories, triumphal games were held that involved gladiator contests, a naval battle on the flooded basin at the Field of Mars, beast-hunts involving 400 lions, and thousands of captives fighting to the death at the Circus Maximus.

Caesar's empire lasted for four more centuries in its unified form and fourteen centuries in the form of its daughter state as the Byzantine Empire. His legacy as a victorious commander is well-earned. But his true esteem by military historians does not come from his success in battle. History is littered with courageous commanders whose empires crumbled shortly after their deaths, such as Genghis Khan, Alexander, and Tamerlane. What distinguished Caesar was making those conquests sustainable through shrewd maneuvering and political acumen. This was not an easy matter, as demonstrated by the shaky alliance of the First Triumvirate. It is a legacy that not even the most able of commanders could leave behind.

Throughout his career Caesar attempted to combine tradition with innovation to strengthen Rome. Historian Daniela Zaharia notes that the old Roman values of liberty (*libertas*) and citizenship (*civitas romana*) had diminished in the age of the civil wars. Caesar ran a political campaign of promising to restore the values of Rome. He built a public persona that embodied these qualities. He portrayed himself as a pious ruler who respected his ancestors. As an innovator he introduced new festivities in the religious calendar of the city. Caesar added himself to the list of those honored, giving himself divine status. There were not religious festivals in honor of a mortal before Julius Caesar but only for the gods, according to antiquarian Varro. This innovation became a rule for imperial religious ceremonies. He also issued coins bearing his own image. His was the first Roman coinage to feature a living individual.

He was recognized as Rome's greatest statesman, even in the decades immediately following his death. The Roman biographer, Plutarch, claims that "if one [were to] compare him with such men as Fabius and Scipio and Metellus, and with the men of his own time or a little before him, like Sulla, Marius, the two Luculli, or even

Pompey himself, whose fame for every sort of military excellence was at this time flowering out and reaching to the skies, Caesar will be found to surpass them all in his achievements."

Caesar's strongest endorsement for his productivity comes from no less than Jesus Christ himself. In the early first century, Jewish religious leaders tried to bait the teacher into a trap. They wanted to end his ministry for fear of him stirring up an Israeli rebellion against Rome and bringing down the imperial sword upon their necks. They asked him if it was incumbent to pay taxes to the Roman Empire, a pagan political entity many Israelites believed would be defeated by the coming Messiah. If he answered 'yes,' Israelites would see him as siding with an unpopular foreign power, and he would lose his support. If he answered 'no,' Jewish religious leaders could tell Rome he was a rebel. Jesus escaped the trap by holding up a denarius to the crowd that bore the visage of Caesar. He enquired as to whose picture was engraved upon it. Receiving his answer, Jesus said, "Render unto Caesar what is Caesar's and unto God what is God's."

Such is the legacy of a man who was so effective during his time on earth that even the founder of Christianity acknowledged that the imperial office he created controlled the political domains of the Earth.

CHAPTER ELEVEN

JUSTINIAN THE GREAT (482-565)

Justinian I of Byzantium was a pivotal figure between the ancient and medieval periods. He rose to imperial power in 527 AD and reacquired Roman lands in Europe that were lost a century before to Vandal and Ostrogothic invasions. He removed the rotting branches of his administration, replacing bureaucrats from the aristocracy with independent counselors. His successes looked to the past glories of the empire but also to the future. Once again the Roman Empire stretched out to the Atlantic Ocean, bringing in vast amounts of tribute from the reconquered territory. But Justinian also rewrote the Roman law, the *Corpus Juris Civilis*. Early in his reign he commissioned a legal expert in his court, Tribonian, to gather together legal commentaries and laws of the Roman legal system into a single text that would hold the force of law. It was composed in Latin and is still the basis of civil law in many of the empire's descendant states.

But the reason for Justinian's far-reaching influence is not for his administrative brilliance or force of character. These qualities allowed him to succeed, but they did not create the initial conditions that allowed him to consolidate his power and easily wipe out his foes. The reason for his successes come from a far more unlikely source. According to one author, Justinian owes his productive genius and influential imperial reign to the bubonic plague. The flea that carried the bacillus created conditions for the formation of modern Europe.

According to William Rosen, author of *Justinian's Flea*, the first severe outbreak of the bubonic plague devastated the Mediterranean world, slashing its labor force, which caused significant changes in wages and worker mobility. Over 100 million died. Historians have made similar arguments about the economic transformations that the 14th-century Black Plague wrought on medieval Europe, but Rosen says such reforms actually began in the 6th century. With a quarter of the population dead, the resulting labor shortage drove up wages and costs for agricultural production and military service.

> Justinian's consolidation and rationalization of Roman law underpins the civil code across the continent. Haghia Sophia, Justinian's great Constantinople church, is one of the wonders of the world. The chaos left by imperial decline turned out to be an incubator for nation-states such as France and Spain. The plague-caused labor shortage spurred technology improvements that boosted agricultural productivity and put Europe on the path to becoming the world's first rich continent.

But the bubonic plague alone cannot account for Justinian's productive abilities. He was able to turn catastrophe into an opportunity for reform. He was obsessed with the idea of restoring the Roman Empire by launching military campaigns of reconquest into West Africa, Italy, and Spain. The official court historian Procopius writes, "Then appeared the emperor Justinian, entrusted by God with this commission, to watch over the whole Roman

Empire, and so far as was possible, to remake it." Justinian designed his realm in the image of an autocratic Roman Empire, but he filled this cast with a Christian mold, resulting in a divinely supported autocracy. His laws were far-reaching but based on a theistic moral grounding, with the church and clergy becoming instruments of imperial power.

Justinian's piety was a major factor in his productive reign. He was by all accounts truly devout, as shown by his interests in theology, spending the final years of his life writing a theological treatise and in discussions with monks. He took for himself the title *isapostolos* (equal with the Apostles), positioning himself as having power within the church and the ability to interpret the teachings of Christ, setting himself above conflict with the church. Justinian's orthodox beliefs freed him of many political problems, as emperors whose beliefs ran contrary to the religious establishment wasted enormous political capital on theological squabbles instead of ruling Byzantium.

A 2014 paper on the psychological aspects of Justinian's personality described the characteristics that made him such an effective reformer. He showed tendencies for self-determination, self-confidence, perfectionism, and autocracy. He was also terribly hard working and paranoid of conspiracies. Harold Lasswell notes he is only one of a small number of leaders who possessed the ability to go long stretches without food or sleep.

Justinian was controlling and lacked enough trust in his subordinates to delegate responsibilities. Procopius writes that he did not allow anyone in the empire to make a decision by himself (although Procopius depicts Justinian as a demon in his *Secret History*, so we should take his descriptions with a bit of skepticism). He involved himself in battlefield decisions and even drew an early sketch of the Haghia Sophia, reportedly based on an angelic vision.

That is not to say that he did not surround himself with intelligent people. Justinian had an extraordinary eye for talent. He appointed Flavius Belisarus as general, who managed to reconquer much of the Western Roman Empire in the sixth century. He did so by leading a small force of 5,000 soldiers against ten times as many Goths. But Justinian realized that Belisarius' popularity threatened to win the hearts of the public, which could weaken the emperor's hold on the throne. Justinian did not give the general a hero's welcome upon his return to Constantinople. He only earned the spite of the emperor, who was deeply jealous of his success. In 562 Belisarius stood trial in Constantinople on charges of corruption. He was found guilty and imprisoned, but the emperor later pardoned him. In an epilogue to Belisarius' life, legend has it that Justinian ordered his eyes to be put out, which reduced him to a homeless beggar near the Pincian Gate of Rome.

Justinian's wife Theodora was an even greater asset. She was a shrewd and intelligent empress who cowed internal and external threats. Theodora was not afraid to wield power, which she did with gusto whenever an official entered her antechamber. According to Edward Gibbon, they had to kiss her feet and carefully follow all rules of royal decorum. If not they were thrown in prison or exiled. Gibbon may have exaggerated her strong will, but she and her husband were not afraid to terrorize their bureaucracy, which they suspected of corruption.

Theodora's will was so strong that Procopius believed that she dominated her weak husband and undermined the office of the emperor. But the historian despised Theodora, and his argument is unconvincing. Theodora strengthened her husband in times of weakness. She urged him to put down the Nika Revolt and make a stand for his imperial right to rule.

Historian Daniela Zaharia writes that the most prominent of Justinian's psychological traits are vigor, great potential to accomplish his goals, morality, and altruism. He had high levels of self-efficacy, the psychological dimension of the self that includes a set of beliefs in one's ability to complete tasks and reach goals. He was a perfectionist, whether at the personal level concerning his piety, or the imperial level of resurrecting the Roman Empire. He also had a high level of social intelligence, and knew how to flash his imperial power in order to show might to Byzantine subjects and cow would-be rebels into submission.

The best-known example is Justinian's rebuilding campaign that he undertook after Constantinople's citizens burned much of the city to the ground in protest against his heavy taxes. To raise the funds for his Italian military campaigns, Justinian's finance minister John of Cappadocia introduced 26 new taxes. Most fell on the wealthy. Anger at the imperial center merged with already-volatile social conditions after Justinian had harshly reacted to fighting between the Greens and the Blues in the capital. These groups were two factions that cheered on chariot racing teams who competed at the Hippodrome, a coliseum within easy walking distance of the Imperial Palace. The Hippodrome held nearly 100,000 spectators.

The Greens resented being rebuffed by the couple. The Blues, who were generally liked by Justinian and Theodora, believed their favor had been withdrawn, so the rulers earned the scorn of both sides. In January 532 rebellion threatened the city. At the next chariot race, the two factions shouted *Nika! Nika!* ("Win! Win!"), normally a cheer for their favorite charioteer, in defiance of the government. During a period of January 11-19, popular outrage crystalized into full-scale rioting.

They poured into Constantinople's inner city. They torched opulent buildings of the capital, including the fourth-century Church of Hagia Sophia, the church in which the royal couple wed. The mob even proclaimed a new emperor, Hypatius, the nephew of former emperor Anastasius I. Several other important religious and imperial buildings were burned, including Hagia Eirene, the Chalke Gate to the imperial palace, and the baths of Zeuxippus.

Justinian thought of exile, but Theodora steeled him against the mob. She gave an impassioned speech concerning the virtues of fighting to maintain power rather than living as an exile: "But consider first whether, when you reach safety, you will regret that you did not choose death in preference. As for me, I stand by the ancient saying: the purple is the noblest winding-sheet." After Justinian gathered courage from her words he ordered his trusted officers Belisarius and Mundus to attack the demonstrators. His Thracian and Gothic troops assaulted the Hippodrome and killed over 30,000 protestors, including the challenger to the throne Hypatius at Theodora's insistence. This number equaled 10 percent of the city's population.

The damage to Constantinople's center allowed Justinian an opportunity to begin a prolific rebuilding campaign. Through urban planning and architectural patronage, he commissioned dozens of churches and public buildings. He rebuilt the Church of the Holy Apostles in Constantinople, which was in a very poor state by the 6th century. The emperor adorned the Great Palace of Constantinople with mosaics. He built a column topped by a bronze statue of himself in the Augustaeum in 543. Many of his palaces and churches still stand.

Through this building program the city reached its full imperial splendor. It remained the envy of the medieval world for centuries. Western Europeans who traveled to the Byzantine capital were shocked by its grandeur. Their home cities were little more than a castle and cathedral surrounded by thatched-roofed cottages. Constantinople was ten times larger than Paris or London in the early Middle Ages. Historians later described it as the still-beating heart of antiquity.

The most magnificent of these works was the Haghia Sophia church, completed in 537. The physicist Isidore of Milteus and mathematician Anthemius of Tralles were the chief architects. They achieved the building's revolutionary design, combining a massive rectangular basilica with a dome resting on pendentives (a constructive device permitting the placing of a circular dome over a square room) and supported by pillars. Materials were brought from all over the world: Hellenistic columns from the Temple of Artemis in Ephesus, large stones from Egypt, green marble from Thessaly, and yellow stone from Syria. Over 10,000 workers constructed the building. Its massive dome set a standard in architecture that had a lasting effect on Byzantine and Islamic religious buildings. It was the largest church in the world and remained so for nearly a millennium. Justinian, upon walking into the church, didn't bother with modesty. He exclaimed, "Oh Solomon, I have surpassed thee!"

His building efforts were not limited to churches and mosaics. Justinian strengthened his borders with fortifications in his eastern and western domains. He also built bridges, courthouses, baths, cisterns, storehouses, and asylums. He ensured that Constantinople had a steady water supply through commissioning massive underground cisterns fed by aqueducts that stretched hundreds of kilometers northeast to nearby forests. To prevent floods from damaging the nearby city of Dara he commissioned an advanced arch dam. The Sangarius Bridge was built in Bithynia to ensure that military supplies could move unencumbered to his western borders.

The emperor found creative ways to grow the Byzantine economy. Although he had access to extensive trade networks throughout the Mediterranean – even trading with England in the 6th century – he could not enforce a trade embargo on the enemy Persians. Their silk products were popular among Constantinople's wealthy class, but they were enormously expensive. They passed through the hands of many traders before reaching Byzantium, vastly inflating the original price. He sought to bypass the Persian land route of silk merchants from India by establishing friendly relations with the Abyssinians, but they still could not compete with Persian merchants in India. Justinian found a solution by granting a monopoly to imperial factories of silk products in 541. In the 550s two Byzantine monks managed to smuggle eggs of silk worms from

Central Asia back to Constantinople. Indigenous production of silk was now possible. Persian traders were marginalized.

The emperor also consolidated the authority of the imperial administration. He eliminated the now-useless office of consul, abandoned the principle of strict separation between civil and military authority, and established precedents for future emperors to tighten imperial control. This led to an autocratic trend in Byzantine politics that grew over the centuries. He demanded that all subordinates be loyal servants of the state. This goal was compromised by Justinian's tolerance of corrupt but efficient tax collectors.

Justinian was more than an administrator, urban planner, and military strategist. In the religious sphere he took a leading role in shaping church policy. As a caesaropapist emperor, he exercised supreme authority over ecclesiastical matters. His education included theological training, an interest he kept all his life. Because Constantinople was Christianity's richest and most powerful city, he was its most powerful Christian, with greater wealth and reach than the pope in Rome. He extinguished the final remnants of Greco-Roman paganism and rooted out heretics such as the Manicheans and Samaritans. Justinian fought with equal vigor against the Christian sects of Arianism and Monophysitism. Ironically, his suppression of Monophysitism – popular among the common people – led to their marginalization on the eastern fringes of the Empire, causing Islam's rapid advance through the populace a century later.

He even used the destruction that the bubonic plague wrought on the empire's economy as an opportunity for innovation. Justinian survived the plague, but up to half of the Byzantine population died. Agriculture production collapsed, threatening to undermine the empire's labor-intensive economy. Armed forces lacked food. Sailors lacked foodstuffs to trade. To compensate, the entire agrarian system was restructured to tie producers closer to the land and protect against any future colossal shocks to the system. It in effect became the early medieval three-field system.

Justinian's ability to consolidate power, marginalize his enemies, commit himself to his goals, spot talent, and win the trust of the populace made him among the most effective rulers of the ancient world. His successors never managed to live up to his reputation. The Byzantine Empire declined in later centuries. Nevertheless, Justinian left behind a template of imperial power that statesmen have tried and mostly failed to copy.

CHAPTER TWELVE

PHILIP II OF SPAIN (1527-1598)

King Philip II of Spain, known as Philip the Prudent, ruled the world's largest empire during the Age of Discovery. He controlled Spain from 1556 and Portugal from 1581 until his death in 1598. While married to Mary I, he was also King of England and Ireland. The Spanish empire ruled the 17 Provinces of the Netherlands, much of South America, all of Central America and Texas, the Philippines, and parts of the African coast. His reign birthed Spain's Golden Age, a period of artistic, musical, and literary flourishing. Although he lost the "invincible Armada" in 1588, Philip held together a global empire through his administrative genius at a time when slow travel made such a task improbably difficult.

He controlled Spain and all its colonies for 55 years, starting in 1543 with his appointment as regent for his father, Holy Roman Emperor Charles V. Charles controlled Germany, parts of Italy, Spain, and Belgium, and much of the new world. His principle for ruling centered on "the defense of the Empire, the propagating of the Holy Faith of Jesus Christ, and the persevering of our peoples in peace and security." This principle was sound in theory, but his son upheld it only with great struggle. Philip's global empire had no common culture, currency, or language. It was a messy patchwork of political institutions and laws. Different parts of it held competing economic strategies and even competing branches of Christianity. It would be as if the United States decided to directly control Mexico, Thailand, and South Africa, but do so through each of those countries' legal systems and languages, and do so with weeks or months' wait time between each government missive.

Philip kept these many plates spinning at once by creating one of the most advanced bureaucratic machines in early modern history. His rule was part of Spain's long march toward modern governance that began with his great-grandparents Ferdinand and Isabella. They weakened the nobles, who had once exercised an almost independent authority from the crown and were much of the reason that a political unification of the Iberian Peninsula had taken centuries. Before these reforms, rural Spain resembled something like Afghanistan or inner-city Los Angeles. Local tyrants, warlords, and gang leaders controlled these regions and enforced laws that were largely crafted for their own benefit. Urban officials rarely intervened. Petty criminals were everywhere. After Ferdinand and Isabella's reforms, highwaymen and robbers that filled Spain's rural areas were brought under control, imprisoned, deported, or executed. Crime rates plummeted throughout the kingdom.

Philip benefitted from this centralized justice system that was relatively free of corruption. Isabella eliminated an entire category of royal counselors that consisted of those with personal connections to the monarch. By doing so she strengthened the body of professional administrators, nobles, and bishops that performed bureaucratic and judicial duties. This reform signaled a rupture with the medieval style of governance that depended on a messy web of political alliances that ultimately connected to the monarch and a

124

few royal advisors. It was replaced with an early modern system of a government bureaucracy that ensured the machinery of the state continued to function smoothly from one ruler to the next. This depersonalized model of government dominated Europe over the coming centuries, and it allowed a certain level of automation. The state would not fall apart if one royal family seized control of the throne or if the queen failed to produce a son.

Philip was born in 1527. The two themes that Charles V emphasized during Philip's childhood were the glorification of Spain and the defense of the Catholic Church – a critical mission when the Protestant Reformation, which had already engulfed England and much of Germany and Hungary threatened to collapse the Catholic church. Despite taking up the mantle at a young age as protector of the faith Philip still had a contentious relationship with the Catholic hierarchy. In 1556 he even declared war against the Papal States and temporarily seized territory there, perhaps in response to Pope IV's anti-Spanish stance.

After ascending the throne, Philip stretched out his military might. Funded by gold from the New World, he grew his empire. Spain became the first domain over which the sun truly never set. He controlled Portugal, the Netherlands, and half of Italy – including Sicily, the Duchy of Milan, and the Kingdom of Naples. He controlled Tunis and Tangier in Africa; and Guinea and Angola further down the coast. He held parts of India and all of the Philippines. In the Western hemisphere he controlled Florida, Brazil, Cuba, Peru, and "New Spain" – the modern American Southwest and all of Central America and Mexico.

Historian Geoffrey Parker studied thousands of documents from the time of Philip II's reign to understand the complexity of running a global empire in the 1500s. At this time an average king's domain was no larger than a few day's riding distance in any direction. A few larger realms such as the Ottoman or the Chinese empires were comparable in size to today's nation-states. But nobody controlled global landholdings when the fastest means of travel was by sail. Weeks or even months could go by before news arrived from a far-flung colony. Decisions took just as long to send back. How did Philip do it?

By marginalizing opposition in his empire.

Early in his reign Philip was subject to separate assemblies. The Cortes in Castile, the assembly in Navarre, and three regional rulers of Aragon each jealously guarded their traditional rights and laws from the time they were separate kingdoms. This made it difficult for Philip to rule Spain and his possession. To solve this problem, he gave authority to local agents appointed by the crown and viceroys that implemented royal instructions. To pacify local nobles, he created the Council of State. Its ostensible purpose was to hold forums in which nobles advised the king on matters of governance, but Philip did not attend it himself. The Council existed more to have nobles believe they had real power and to vent their arguments against one another. Realms of the Empire were run by professional administrators who were trained lawyers. They were instruments of state control that did not muddle orders with opinion or disagreement. By these means, Philip was ultimately in charge of the direct administration of his empire. He could fire off orders with little political friction

Parker describes how Philip delegated his many responsibilities. State ministers received orders to send their correspondence to the proper central institution in whatever nation they were located. Council secretaries received great power to resolve state business. For example, the king instructed his viceroys in Italy to direct all matters relating to administration, justice, the patrimony and revenues of the crown and treasury, and other routine affairs to the newly created council of Italy. Matters of war or peace and relations with other rulers were directed to the council of State. A memorandum from the 1570s on allocating incoming business between different councils contained 326 categories, each with its own administrative procedure. The Ministers in America received orders to streamline their correspondence with the council of the Indies, so that "everything that you used to write in many letters, you will now condense into four [categories], according to their contents: administration, justice, war and finance."

Treasure fleets from America delivered literal tons of gold and silver, and the administration of these wealthy colonies was a priority for Philip. This administration was governed by the Council for the Indies, which had a president and eight councilors. It was the Supreme Law Court, and the organization through which the crown imposed its authority on the territory originally conquered by private individuals, the *conquistadores*. There were 10 *Audencias*, or judicial and administrative bodies. These bodies and other local officials had much independence, a vital issue since travel between Madrid and the Americas took a minimum of six weeks.

But the volume of incoming papers continued to rise. Philip had to write or authorize an estimated 1,600 letters a month to keep up with the never-ending problems within his empire. The Council of War only produced two or three bundles of working papers a year in 1560 but turned out over 30 bundles by the 1590s. To quell the near-impossible workload he came up with another administrative innovation. Between 1566 and 1572, Cardinal Diego de Espinosa acted as an alter ego of Philip II – another king in the court who reviewed everything of importance. He recommended important actions and even gave orders on the king's behalf. In 1571, in the run-up to a massive naval battle against the Ottomans, the cardinal reviewed all reports coming from Italy and recommended appropriate actions in the naval campaign, which culminated in Spanish, Italian, and Papal victory against the Ottomans in the Battle of Lepanto. This was the first major naval defeat of the Ottomans, who threatened to conquer the entire Mediterranean Sea.

It is for this and three other reasons that Philip was such a highly productive monarch, Parker writes. First, his network of communications and intelligence network overcame problems imposed by distance and time; second, he chose productive means to formulate and achieve strategic goals; and third, Philip had clear strategic priorities, allowing him to directly address whatever problem came along.

Philip's communication system worked better and faster than that of any of his rivals. His couriers could cover up to 185 kilometers per day. He frequently received European information before his rivals did. He personally visited many of Spain's European possessions, and had enough maps, plans, drawings, surveys, and questionnaires at hand to make him the best-informed monarch of the age. Information from his trans-oceanic colonies was less consistent and more expensive to obtain. But it was better than what most his rivals had, for whom the New World was mostly *terra incognita.*

His subjects were largely obedient to his command style because they believed that Philip exercised his authority through established constitutional channels, not by whim. They were right. On one occasion he sent back a set of orders unsigned, since "it seems to me that there are problems, because those for the three kingdoms of the crown of Aragon, and especially the one for Aragon itself, will not be obeyed and are against the local customs." He pointed out that all royal letters for his eastern kingdoms should be issued by the council of Aragon, and he ordered them to be redrafted. His subjects came to love him for his sense of justice. Parker recalls that when Philip returned to Madrid in 1583, after an absence of three years in Portugal, the crowds that poured out of the city stretched over a mile from the palace, with many men and women at the windows and on the roofs to cheer the monarch.

He succeeded in building a productive empire by earning the trust of his subject. He traveled unarmed through crowded streets despite seven assassination attempts during his long reign. He ate the fresh catch from local fishermen and drank cups of water offered by subjects. He always worked with his study door open and fell to his knees whenever a religious procession passed him on the street, the same as anyone else among the crowd. Philip boasted, "Let tyrants fear: I have always so behaved myself, that under God I have placed my chiefest strength and safeguard in the loyal hearts and goodwill of my subjects."

Philip had to use all of his talents to keep Spain's many enemies at bay. His three foreign adversaries were England, France, and the Ottoman Empire, an Islamic power that controlled the Mediterranean, the Balkan Peninsula, Asia Minor, Egypt, and the coasts of northern Africa. The Ottomans conquered Cyprus and Malta in the early 16th century. As such Philip joined the Holy League, anti-Ottoman coalition organized by Pope Pius V that included the Papal States and Venice. The fleet fought the Ottoman navy at the Battle of Lepanto in 1571. In five hours of fighting on the coast of western Greece, the Catholic maritime states decisively defeated the main fleet of the Ottoman Empire. Philip ended the Islamic empire's domination of the Mediterranean with a 1578 peace treaty that lasted until the end of his reign.

Philip attempted to control England through marriage. He exchanged nuptials with Queen Mary I in 1554, but she died two years later. He then attempted to wed Elizabeth I upon her accession to the throne, but the young sovereign had a force of will equal to that of Philip and was as devout in her Protestantism as he was in his Catholicism. She then encouraged revolt in the Low Countries. He then supported the cause of Mary, Queen of Scots, but Elizabeth signed off on her execution, ending the possibility of a Catholic insurgency against the Tudor dynasty. With the defeat of the Spanish Armada in 1588, English corsairs could pillage Spain's colonies and even Spain's own coasts. Philip's designs on England came to nothing.

Despite these foreign policy setbacks, Philip accomplished his goals with a focused personality. He had little use for moderation.

He was tenacious, industrious, serious, devoted to study, a patron of the arts, gentle to his friends, and pious. He was a devout Catholic and a lover of justice. In 1571, he pardoned prisoners in Spain and the Indies to celebrate the birth of his son and heir. In 1580, he freed prisoners en route to his new kingdom of Portugal.

But this sense of justice compelled him to brutally suppress Protestantism, particularly in the Netherlands. Philip used the Spanish Inquisition to persecute heretics of any stripe and centralize power under the monarchy. During the decade of 1566-76, he executed over 1,200 of his Low Countries' subjects in the early years of the Dutch Revolt. To these, he was cold, secretive, suspicious, and unforgiving. He believed the best way to oppose "heresy" was through force. Philip was a man of his time and an absolutist. To Protestants he was the "demon of the south" (*daemon meridanius*) but to his subjects he was "the prudent king" (*el rey prudente*).

Like any great leader, Philip had faults in his governing style. Later in his reign he outsourced fewer decisions and believed that he should be fully informed of every situation. This obsession with detail came from a growing distrust of his close associates, even members of his immediate family. He was consumed with matters of state, nuances of grammar, building plans, and titles used in court. He worked grueling hours to handle all these matters but apparently took masochistic pleasure in them. When one minister apologized, saying, "I am sorry to fatigue your Majesty with such trifling matters," he replied, "They do not fatigue me, they delight me!"

Yet Philip was able to persevere through difficulty due to his great piety, for better or worse. Philip suffered great crises at the end of his reign, notably the destruction of the Armada in 1588 and the crisis of Aragon in 1591, in which the realm revolted against him. Whenever anything went wrong, the king would blame God for having willed the matter to work against him. But he saw failure or even complete defeat as proof that God was testing him. Such tests confirmed to Philip that the best response was to remain resolute. It is perhaps for this reason that he appeared so dignified to his subjects. One of Philip's earliest biographers confirmed that "brave men who had withstood a thousand dangers trembled in his presence, and no one looked on him without emotion." The same writer commented on his incredible self-control. When Venetian ambassador Leonardo Dona told the king in a public audience in 1573 that Venice had defected without warning from its Spanish alliance and made peace with the Turks, he noticed in amazement that Philip listened to the terms impassively – except that "his mouth made a very small, ironic movement, smiling thinly."

But he cannot be wholly blamed for obsession with details. Philip ruled in the mold of a late medieval/early modern sovereign. Despite creating a massive state bureaucracy, he insisted on making as many important decisions in person as possible. He demonstrated power with an unwillingness to compromise. Although he had talented subordinates as administrators and military commanders, Philip appointed those who tended to agree with his strategic viewpoints. He eventually lost his ability to craft long-term strategy with his "incorrigible urge to meddle."

Philip's massive landholdings were also his undoing. He had to constantly shift attention, whether to Ottoman pirates in the Mediterranean, Dutch rebels, French Protestants, or potential dissidents in the New World. He had dynastic, political, diplomatic, military, social, and economic concerns that intruded on his everyday policies. Even though he was the richest European ruler of his age because of influxes of gold from across the Atlantic, frequent wars threatened Spain with bankruptcy, even to the point that Philip sold his wife's jewelry in 1588. When he died in 1598, he left behind a weakened conglomerate of states divided by culture and religion and economically unstable.

Despite his flaws, Philip was the leader his empire needed. He held together a highly unstable confederation for five decades, running a clean administration despite the incredible workload. He instituted revolutionary government policies that did not become commonplace among other European governments for another century. Although he failed in fiscal prudence and Spain's long wars against France and England, he has earned his reputation as a masterfully prolific ruler of Spain during its golden age.

CHAPTER THIRTEEN

NAPOLEON BONAPARTE (1769-1821)

Numerous contradictions surround the life of Napoleon Bonaparte, widely considered to be the greatest military commander in modern history. He challenged the ancient regimes of Europe and permanently altered the political order of the continent. He placed nations such as Italy, Germany, and Poland on a reform trajectory toward democratic rule and civil rights. Yet he did so by assuming untold-levels of autocratic power by running roughshod over his opponents. His military crusade failed and he reduced France to a second-tier power in Europe's political theatre. By the end of his reign France was beaten, isolated, occupied, dominated, and loathed. But the sheer magnitude of Napoleon's accomplishments made him widely considered to be the most successful military leader in history.

Napoleon's greatest legacies were battlefield strategies that played a prominent role in European military strategy from the late 18th century until the invention of the rifled musket in the mid-19th century. His tactics relied on a highly efficient military machine. It required the intense drilling of soldiers, speedy battlefield movement, and combined arms assaults between infantry, cavalry, and artillery, bayonet charges, short-ranged flintlock musket fire, and a small number of cannons.

Napoleon emerged on France's national military stage in 1795 when he quelled a Royalist revolt of counter-revolutionaries in Paris, lining up artillery to stop the attack. For preventing the revolt, he was rewarded by the French Directory, France's governing body, and gained a new patron in its leader, Paul Barras. Shortly afterwards, he married Josephine de Beauharnais.

The young officer quickly rose through the ranks of the French army, largely owing to his intellectual ability and powerful memory. According to a story from his campaign of 1805, a subordinate was not able to locate his division. Napoleon's aids searched through maps and papers to assist him. But Napolean was able to tell the officer his unit's present location, where he would be stationed for the next three nights, his unit's strength, and the subordinate's military record. This was despite the subordinate being one of 200,000 soldiers with units constantly on the move.

Despite taking command at a young age, Napoleon stepped onto the battlefield fully prepared to lead his troops. He readied himself by devouring hundreds of volumes of military history. Later in his career, Napoleon boasted that his extensive study made him a fully formed battle commander before he ever ordered any troops to attack. He once claimed, "I have fought sixty battles and I have learned nothing which I did not know at the beginning. Look at Caesar; he fought the first like the last."

In 1796, Napoleon commanded the first of his international campaigns in Italy. He took over a poorly equipped and exhausted army that was completely dispirited. They were, however, an experienced group, and Napoleon was able to turn around their fortunes by properly supplying them. More importantly, he gave them better incentives to fight. He distributed promotions based on merit, talent, and elections among peers rather than a prestigious background or connections to the aristocracy.

Napoleon introduced many other innovations into battle. Before the French Revolution, European armies were quite small. They were poorly organized, attacked enemy positions in one long line, and moved sluggishly. But mass conscription swelled the ranks of the Republican army. These conscript mobs didn't have the training to hold a single line while under attack, and it could be easily broken anyway. Napoleon made significant contributions to the structure of national armies by dividing them between infantry brigades, cavalry brigades, corps artillery, and the engineer train.

He used the army corps as a replacement for the division as the army's main organization. Each of these corps was something of a miniature army, consisting of infantry, artillery, and cavalry. Numbering only 10,000 to 30,000, it was a flexible arrangement compared to the lumbering juggernauts that made up Europe's other armies. Such an arrangement could hold off a larger army until help arrived. An entire fighting force did not need to march together; therefore, military logistics were far simpler and allowed for surprise attacks. Each corps could quickly come to the aid of another in battle, or quickly exploit a weakness in enemy lines. The principle was to march divided, but to fight united.

Beyond reforming the structure of the army, Napoleon was the greatest logistician of his age. Napoleon approached military logistics as a science rather than an ad hoc affair. The medieval and early modern legacy of European military logistics was a sloppy approach that depended on purchasing food stuffs from villages, hoping they had enough on hand to feed an army. Food went bad quickly. An army without enough provisions usually disbanded. To this Napoleon famously said that "an army moves on its stomach." He improved the French supply chain to a level of factory efficiency. Ideas he invented include the canned ration – allowing food to travel for weeks or months without spoiling – the supply depot, and the mobile field ambulance.

In 1798, the Five Directors had considered invading England, but Napoleon convinced them to invade Egypt and cut off English trade routes instead. He defeated the Mamluks, a provincial Ottoman-backed dynasty that essentially ruled Egypt, at the Battle of the Pyramids. Unfortunately, he found that his concerns with the British were correct when his fleet was defeated by the Royal Navy on the Nile. Napoleon then invaded Syria to gain control over the Ottoman Empire, but was unsuccessful in his siege of Acre.

Without receiving orders to do so, Napoleon decided to return to France after he saw that his replacement had lost northern Italy in the War of the Second Coalition. France was bankrupt; the popularity of the Directory waned. Napoleon was unquestionably the most popular figure in the country due to his meteoric rise and sterling military career. He was recruited by one of the Directors, Emmanuel Joseph Sieyes, to overthrow the government. Napoleon maneuvered into being elected as First Consul. He assumed legal power as well, and wrote the Constitution of the Year VIII. The general from Corsica was now the leader of France.

Napoleon was as productive as a head of state as he was a military commander. He instituted drastic and far-reaching reforms to the French government, which had already transformed considerably in the previous two decades. He created a centralized banking system, a university system, tax reforms, and public works. He also created the Napoleonic Code, which institutionalized ideas from the French Revolution by weakening feudal tradition and the power of the aristocracy. It removed birthright privileges, created freedom of religion in the Catholic-dominated country, and established career placement in the government bureaucracy based on merit. This legal code was created by second consul Jean Jacques Regis de Cambaceres but with major influence from Bonaparte himself.

Napoleon returned to Italy in 1800 to once again defeat the Austrians. After the battle of Marengo, he drove them completely out of Italy. He reached a peace agreement with the British when they signed the Treaty of Amiens in 1801, as both nations tired of war. In the Western Hemisphere, however, the French faced an unexpected uprising in the African slave-dominated island Haiti in 1803. Napoleon decided that defending any French territory in North America would be almost impossible. He sold the Louisiana Territory to the United States, thus filling his treasury and preventing his army from being overextended across the globe.

Napoleon was named Emperor on May 18, 1804; his coronation took place six months later. During this time he launched the Napoleonic Wars, a series of military conflicts that pitted the French Empire against numerous European powers that were forced into various coalitions. He first struck Britain on May 18, 1803, ending the one-year-old Peace of Amiens. The British were reluctant to fight France again after the disastrous 1799-1802 War of the Second Coalition but realized the danger that the French emperor posed to the rest of the continent. They formed the Fifth Coalition with Russia and Austria to check his spread.

For years they were helpless to stop him. Napoleon implemented strategic, tactical, and logistic reforms that defined the way the most destructive wars in history were fought. Regarding the innovations that he brought to the battlefield, there were three main military strategies that undergirded Napoleon's battle philosophy, as noted by military historian Peter Dean. The first was *la maneuver sur les derrieres,* in which the enemy was pinned by a feint attack before the French army marched by a hidden route to attack the enemy's rear flank. Napoleon's opponents spent more than a decade to learn of a countermeasure.

The second innovation was to favor a central position when encountering two or more enemy armies. This allowed him to engage each enemy separately, thus defeating more powerful forces.

During the Waterloo campaign, Napoleon attacked Blucher's Prussians while Marshal Ney's corps dealt with Wellington's Anglo-Dutch army. The third maneuver was strategic penetration. This involved smashing the enemy's corridor of defenses, followed by a rapid march deep into enemy territory to seize a city or town and use it as a base of operations for the next step of the campaign. To launch this attack, he used massed artillery to open up enemy defenses. Rather than scatter cannons throughout the infantry, he combined all of a corps' artillery into a single unit. They would concentrate fire on one point, blowing a hole in the enemy line and allowing the rest of the army to move through.

In 1806 Napoleon reached what many military historians consider to be the apogee of his military career. He defeated the Austrians and Ulm at the Battle of Austerlitz, also known as the Battle of Three Emperors. The Austrians were forced once again to surrender. Before the battle, Napoleon was not confident in his ability to defeat the coalition of Tsar Alexander I and Holy Roman Emperor Francis II. He could only muster 72,000 men and 157 guns, while the Allies had 85,000 troops and 318 guns. The Allies planned to use their superior forces to strike France's right flank and launch a diversionary attack against the left.

Napoleon crafted a brilliant plan to counter this strategy. He shrugged off all suggestions from his advisors for retreat and lured the Allies to attack on his right flank by deliberately weakening it. This caused the Allied forces to leave the Pratzen Heights vulnerable in order to move to the right side. He then launched a surprise counterattack in the center by concealing his forces opposite the Pratzen Heights. His troops attacked and recaptured the Heights, then launched an assault on the center of the Allied Army, delivering a debilitating strike, and encircling them from the rear.

The French successfully defeated the Allies and ended the Third Coalition. In the aftermath of the battle, the Allies suffered over 27,000 casualties out of an army of 73,000. They lost 180 guns and

50 standards. The French lost 9,000 out of their 67,000 troops. France secured an amazing victory despite teetering on the brink of financial collapse days before. Tsar Alexander commented on the battle with the following lamentation: "We are babies in the hands of a giant." The Holy Roman Emperor abdicated, his millennium-old empire ceased to exist, and the Confederation of the Rhine, a buffer zone of states between France and Germany, was created.

Napoleon could win these lopsided victories because he understood better than any leader of his age that productive leadership came through charisma and psychology. He often secured victory in battle through his tremendous force of personality. At the Battle of Arcole in 1796, seeing his troops falter against the Austrians, he grabbed a French flag, ran to the front, and waved it to motivate them to continue the attack. The French still lost, but such performances earned him considerable respect among rank-and-file troops. His enormous confidence inspired others, and he knew the impact that morale had on warfare. Napoleon said that, "morale is to the physical as three is to one." Another time he asked the commander of a veteran regiment who the bravest soldier in his unit was. When Napoleon received the answer, he walked up to the soldier, removed his own Legion of Honor medal, and pinned it to the man's lapel.

He secured his troops' loyalty by commanding their obedience to his charismatic person. His belief in the mystical power of charisma evolved into the French concept of *élan vital* – a fighting spirit assumed to be instilled in every Frenchman, capable of turning back any enemy because of its power. Such blind faith in *élan vital* led to France's disastrous losses against Germany in the early battles of World War I.

At this point in his career, Napoleon's weaknesses as a commander bubbled to the surface. His obsession with military affairs turned him into a micromanager. He promoted soldiers who had flourished under his command but operated poorly as independent officers. Napoleon's inability to keep other European powers divided or adapt to the more violent nature of warfare in the early nineteenth century led to his eventual downfall. He fought wars of attrition against Russia that massively reduced his troop strength from half a million to 40,000. He attempted to perpetuate a political legacy by founding the House of Bonaparte, an imperial and royal European dynasty in which his family members were installed on the thrones of European client states. They held power for a decade in Italy, Spain, Westphalia, Holland, and Naples. But by the end of the Napoleonic Wars the dynasty collapsed under its own weight.

Napoleon was told by his advisors to abdicate as emperor, which he agreed to do on the condition that his son could be appointed to the throne. This was unacceptable to the allies. He was exiled to the island of Elba but returned to France in March of 1815 to reclaim the throne. For 100 days, he once again held power. Napoleon marched his army toward Belgium, where he defeated the Prussian army of Gebhard Leberecht von Blucher. He then directed his army towards Waterloo to attack the British army, led by the Duke of Wellington. When the battle ended and his devastating losses were made manifest, Napoleon's career as general and emperor ended.

Napoleon abdicated once again and spent his remaining years exiled on the British island of Saint-Helena, over 1,000 miles from the west coast of Africa. Here he wrote his memoirs and suffered under poor treatment from his captors. His health began to fail. According to his autopsy, he ultimately succumbed to stomach cancer. The once-great emperor died on May 5, 1821.

His legacy is so far reaching that it is difficult to summarize, but it was universally recognized, even by his bitterest enemies. When the Duke of Wellington was asked after Waterloo who he thought to be the greatest general of all time, he said "in this age, in past ages, in any age, Napoleon." Napoleon Bonaparte forever changed France and Europe. As both a brilliant and determined leader of government, he established a legal code that is still used to this day;

adopted the metric system; terminated the Holy Roman Empire's millennium-long influence on the European continent; implemented greater religious tolerance in his European client states; and permanently curtailed the power of the French aristocracy in favor of its citizens. However, what he had not done was achieve his grand strategy of building a French Empire that would control Europe and the Middle East.

Despite his failings, Napoleon's accomplishments in life were nearly unparalleled. He was a remarkably productive general, statesman, and commander. His actions saved the French Republic. Although his legacy remains controversial today – the French either consider him a power-hungry ogre or leader of a golden age that built enduring democratic institutions – his legacy casts a long shadow over Western civilization.

CHAPTER FOURTEEN

THEODORE ROOSEVELT (1858-1919)

In the late 1800s, a doctor visited a wealthy couple in New York to examine their sickly son, then a university student. He was severely asthmatic, a condition often fatal in those days. Dr. Dudley Sargent told the young man that due to this condition and his weak heart, failure to lead a quiet life would result in death.

Theodore Roosevelt's father disagreed with this diagnosis. He took his son aside and told him that sitting idly in one's weakness was no way to live. He said, "Theodore, you have the mind but you have not the body, and without the help of the body the mind cannot go as far as it should. I am giving you the tools, but it is up to you to make your body."

His son agreed. After Dr. Sargent told him the grim prognosis, young Theodore shot back as follows: "Doctor, I'm going to do all the things you tell me not to do. If I've got to live the sort of life you have described, I don't care how short it is."

Roosevelt made good on his word. He and his father built a gym in his house, where he practiced weight lifting and boxing. Roosevelt soon developed a rugged physique and established a lifelong habit of exercise and purposefully straining himself. He joined the rowing team at Harvard. During his European honeymoon a year after graduation, he took a detour and scaled the 15,000-foot Matterhorn in Switzerland. Other work experiences that required physical hardiness were cattle rancher, deputy sheriff, explorer, war hero, and police commissioner. He loved boxing and won Harvard's intramural lightweight championship. Roosevelt continued to spar throughout his political career, even during his days in the White House. One day he boxed a young artillery officer, who smashed a blood vessel in his eye. Roosevelt remained nearly blind in his left eye for the rest of his life.

His unusual level of vigor animated other seasons of his life. In 1898 the Spanish-American War broke out, and Roosevelt volunteered as a commander for the U.S. Volunteer Cavalry, known as the Rough Riders. He led a charge on Kettle Hill at the Battle of San Juan Hill and return to the United States as a war hero. Roosevelt parlayed this fame into a campaign for governor of New York, which he won. At the time New York was run by the state's political machine, and its bosses did not want to deal with the headache of Roosevelt's proposed reforms. They "promoted" him to the vice presidency under William McKinley in order to neutralize him. To their surprise, and everyone else's, McKinley won the presidency but was assassinated in 1901. The young upstart Roosevelt was now at age 42 the youngest president in American history.

Although many aspects of his personality made him the highly productive man he became, the most important was that Roosevelt seized initiative. According to a colleague, his motto was "action, action, and more action." He took the reins of whatever task he chose. Once he determined the correct course of action, Roosevelt moved rapidly. Theodore Roosevelt understood the value of taking the initiative from his study of military history. The first mover held the advantages, set the terms of engagement, and could surprise an enemy who rested on his laurels.

An episode from 1884 illustrates this trait. His wife died in childbirth, and his mother died of typhoid on the same day in the same house. To begin a new chapter in his life he moved West to work as a cowboy. A man had intentions on Roosevelt's ranch. He hired a killer named Paddock to get rid of him. Hearing of this, Roosevelt armed himself and rode over to Paddock's residence to end the situation immediately. He said: "I understand you have threatened to kill me on sight. I have come over to see when you want to begin the killing."

Paddock did not bother him again.

A second factor in Roosevelt's productivity and versatility was his omnivorous reading habits. Roosevelt read frequently due to his belief that efficiency did not come from packing in scheduled activities down to every last minute of the day; rather, it was through the regular feeding of his intellect. Even during the height of a presidential campaign, he packed in nearly four hours of reading a day. He enjoyed works of fiction, science, political philosophy, and history. One can imagine a nervous political aide bursting in his study, telling Roosevelt to put down his copy of Cicero because he was scheduled to begin the day's fourth speech in only two minutes.

This attitude is reflected in his daily routine. When he was nominated for the vice presidency in 1900, after the previous Vice President Garret Hobart died, he campaigned for William McKinley. Here is an outline of his daily schedule.

7:00 AM	Breakfast
7:30 AM	A speech
8:00 AM	Reading a historical work
9:00 AM	A speech

10:00 AM	Dictating letters
11:00 AM	Discussing Montana mines
11:30 AM	A speech
12:00 PM	Reading an ornithological work
12:30 PM	A speech
1:00 PM	Lunch
1:30 PM	A speech
2:30 PM	Reading Sir Walter Scott
3:00 PM	Answering telegrams
3:45 PM	A speech
4:00 PM	Meeting the press
4:30 PM	Reading
5:00 PM	A speech
6:00 PM	Reading
7:00 PM	Supper
8-10 PM	Speaking
11:00 PM	Reading alone in his car
12:00 AM	To bed.

Aside from reading much, Roosevelt read from a wide variety of subjects. He enjoyed Sir Walter Scott and ornithology along with historical anthologies or Greek classics. He always carried a book with him, whether enforcing the law in the Dakota Badlands or sitting in the Oval Office. Throughout his life, Roosevelt read an average of five books a week.

A more shallow approach to learning would dictate that one only read books in his or her profession or chosen field. Roosevelt would have taken a bayonet to such an idea. His diverse reading made him informed on nearly any subject in conversation. It also allowed him to add creativity to whatever job he held. Roosevelt's knowledge of the natural world, for example, influenced his decision to create the United States Forest Service and establish five new national parks.

He began the Wildlife Refuge System and set aside 42 million acres for national forests and areas of special interest, such as the Grand Canyon.

He was also a prolific author. Roosevelt's first book was "The Naval War of 1812," written to great acclaim when he was 23 years old, earning him a reputation as a respectable historian. He wrote 37 other books, including a biography of Oliver Cromwell, a history of New York City, the four-volume series "The Winning of the West," and an autobiography. He also wrote numerous magazine articles and books about hunting or his adventures on the frontier. Outside of his published works he produced more than 150,000 letters.

Roosevelt was not a completely self-made man. He had a near-photographic memory and enormous mental powers. As a child he was homeschooled and absorbed everything his parents and tutors fed him. His biographer Edmund Morris cited several cases in which he could recite poetry over a decade after reading it. He could dictate letters and memos to two separate secretaries while reading a book at the same time.

But above all his productivity must be credited to his great resilience. One of the most famous examples of his tenacity was suffering an assassination attempt at a campaign event, then proceeding to give an hour-and-a-half-long speech. The story goes that an assassin, an unemployed saloonkeeper, trailed him for three weeks through eight states during the 1912 presidential election in which Roosevelt was a candidate for the newly-formed Bull Moose Party. As he entered his car outside the Gilpatrick Hotel, Roosevelt stood up in the open-air vehicle and waved his hat to the crowd. The assassin saw his chance, took out his Colt revolver, and fired. The bullet hit Roosevelt and ran three inches into his chest after passing through a jacket pocket containing his steel eyeglass case and copy of his 50-page speech, which was folded in half. Although blood seeped into Roosevelt's shirt, he concluded as an anatomist that the bullet had not penetrated the chest wall into his lung because he was not coughing blood. He continued to walk to the auditorium and mounted the podium.

"Ladies and gentleman, I don't know whether you fully understand that I have just been shot." He then shocked the audience by unbuttoning his vest to reveal the bloodstained shirt "....but it takes more than that to kill a Bull Moose." He then reached into his coat pocket and pulled out the bullet-torn speech. "Fortunately I had my manuscript, so you see I was going to make a long speech, and there is a bullet -- there is where the bullet went through -- and it probably saved me from it going into my heart. The bullet is in me now, so I cannot make a very long speech, but I will try my best."

He orated for the next 90 minutes. Roosevelt's nervous aides begged him to stop speaking and tried to surround him at the podium to catch him if he passed out. They backed off when he shot daggers at them. By the end of the speech his voice weakened and his breath shortened, but only at its conclusion did he agree to go to the hospital. Even before he gave the speech, Roosevelt demanded that the crowd not hurt his would-be assassin and bring him over for an interrogation. "Don't hurt him. Bring him here. I want to see him." Roosevelt then asked the shooter, "What did you do it for?" With no answer coming, he said, "Oh, what's the use? Turn him over to the police."

Roosevelt's energy and force of will caused him to expand the scope and power of the presidency. He wanted to make the United States a global force, which at the time was only a junior partner to the nations of Europe. He led efforts to secure rights to build the Panama Canal. Roosevelt even visited the site personally, making him the first sitting president to leave the United States. He also increased the powers of the Monroe Doctrine and established America as the policeman of the Western Hemisphere, sending a warning to any would-be colonizers or troublemakers attempting political mischief south of U.S. borders. But he ultimately believed in diplomacy over war, personally negotiating peace between Russia and Japan, earning a Nobel Peace Prize for his efforts.

A final reason for his productivity is less interesting but no less important: Roosevelt was an early riser who accomplished the most important duties of the day first. He co-led a disastrous expedition across the Amazon basin in 1913-1914 after his presidency concluded. Although he only ate half rations despite the back-breaking labor of carrying canoes over land and enduring sweltering heat, even suffering bouts of malaria, Roosevelt still found time to write. He raised funds for the expedition on the condition that he would provide a written account of the journey. These accounts formed the basis of his book *Through the Brazilian Wilderness*. Despite the difficulties of the expedition, Roosevelt woke up before the rest of the camp, went for his morning swim (making sure that the water was free of piranhas), then wrote a quota of pages.

He wrote in the jungle for two reasons: first, the details of the expedition would have been lost if he had waited to write from the comfort of his home in America. Second, he knew that writing in the beginning of the day gave him energy that would not be available if he waited until nightfall. Any writer can attest that the excuses for not writing are much more compelling at night than in the morning.

While Roosevelt possessed far more physical and mental energy than the average person, his lessons of productivity are many and worth considering today. Above all, he would advocate continuous action and forward movement. The worst thing for a man to do, he said, was not to make the wrong decision, but be fraught with indecision. "Far better is it to dare mighty things, to win glorious triumphs, even though checkered by failure... than to rank with those poor spirits who neither enjoy nor suffer much, because they live in a gray twilight that knows not victory nor defeat."

PART IV

PHILOSOPHERS AND THEOLOGIANS

CHAPTER FIFTEEN

IBN SINA (980-1037)

"The ink of a scholar is more holy than the blood of a martyr."
So goes the hadith, a saying of Islam ascribed to Muhammed. It was
also an apt description of the scholar Ibn Sina (known as
"Avicenna" in Europe). Born in 980 in Central Asia, he is the most
important Islamic philosopher of the pre-modern era. His medical
treatise *The Canon of Medicine* (al-Qanun fi'l-Tibb) was a standard
medical textbook in Europe and the Middle East until 1650. It
included all the medical and pharmacological knowledge of his time.
It considers over 750 different drugs, with comments on their
application and effectiveness. There are quite modern ideas found in
this medieval medical book. Ibn Sina discusses the importance of
dietetics, the benefits of anesthesia in surgery, and the influence of
climate and environment on health. He was even an oncologist – Ibn
Sina advised surgeons to remove cancer in its earliest stages and
recommended experimentation on animals before humans.

He lived during the golden age of the Abbasid Empire. In the ninth and tenth centuries, it was considered by many historians to have been the site of the cultural and scientific golden age of Islam. The Middle East was the medieval world's center for scholarship and science; Europe had barely emerged from the fall of the Roman Empire centuries earlier.

The Abbasids established their capital of Baghdad as the global center of learning and scholarship. Baghdad sat at the crossroads of Eurasia and regained its status as the world's center for philosophy, science, and medicine. Many texts from the ancient world were assembled and translated into Arabic at the House of Wisdom, the world's first scientific venture. Were it not for this endeavor, ancient Greek texts would have most likely been lost. Philosophy and science were discovered and rediscovered, including geometry, algebra (an Arabic word in origin), and the algorithm (also an Arabic word).

Many brilliant scholars were active at this time, but Ibn Sina stood above them all. His most important philosophical work was *The Book of Healing*, a book about the self's existence in this world and an argument for God as the Necessary Existence. Despite its title, it is not concerned with medicine but intended to "heal" ignorance of the soul. It is a multi-volume scientific and philosophical encyclopedia. In the book, God is presented as the foundation for his theories of the soul, intellect, and cosmos. The book is divided into four parts: natural sciences, logic, mathematics, and metaphysics. *The Book of Healing* was translated into Latin in the late 12th century in Spain, spreading to Paris only a few years later. It had major impact on Thomas Aquinas and the development of medieval scholasticism.

His output as a scholar was mind-boggling, considering that ink and paper were almost luxury items. Ibn Sina wrote 450 different works. They covered a wide array of subjects including astronomy, alchemy, geology, geography, psychology, Islamic theology, mathematics, logic, physics, and poetry. Some individual books were encyclopedic in length. *The Book of Healing* was an enormously ambitious attempt to provide a comprehensive account of all human knowledge and systematically categorize it. The book is considered to be among the longest books ever written by a single author. It provides both practical and theoretical information and covers logic, the natural sciences, mathematics, metaphysics, and theology. Within each of these sections are numerous sub-sections. For example, mathematics is divided into four sections – music, arithmetic, astronomy, and geometry – with each section further sub-divided.

Like many of the other highly prolific people mentioned in this book, Ibn Sina had a privileged upbringing but was mostly self-taught. His father Abdullah led the Bukharan government's tax department, which required him to master algebra, statistics, mathematics, and the Indian number system. He took his son along with him on travels and imparted basic information to him. Ibn Sina committed the entire Qur'an to memory by the age of 10. He learned arithmetic from an Indian greengrocer. Abdullah realized his son's intellectual potential and provided him with a philosophy tutor.

Ibn Sina learned basic mathematics, natural sciences, and theology from his teachers but quickly surpassed them. He taught himself medicine and became an accomplished doctor by the age of 16, even discovering new methods of treatment through his frequent attendance to the sick. For the next several years he soaked up knowledge. From ages 16 to 18 he read philosophy constantly, never getting a full night's sleep during these years. Whenever he encountered an obstacle in his studies he left his books, performed ablutions before prayer, then went to the mosque, and continued in prayer until he understood the matter. He continued his studies late into the night and even worked out these problems in his sleep. In order to understand Aristotle, he read *Metaphysics* forty times until the works were imprinted in his memory. But he could not understand it until a bookseller provided him with a commentary by al-Farabi.

His aptitude for self-study allowed him to work different professions for different patrons throughout his life. Ibn Sina achieved full status as a qualified physician at age 18. With his newly-acquired medical skills he helped to cure Nuh ibn Mansur, the sultan of Bukhara. The sultan enrolled Ibn Sina in his service and gave him access to his library. After his patron died in 997, Ibn Sina left Central Asia and spent much of his life in the courts of provincial rulers of the Abbasid Caliphate. At these courts he held different political offices, advising sovereigns on matters of administration, war, diplomacy, and economic policy. The final 10 years of his life were spent in the Persian city of Isfahan, where he accompanied Abu Ya'far 'Ala Addaula on military campaigns as a physician and general literary and science advisor.

Ibn Sina remained a prolific author despite his time-consuming professional duties. When he left Bukhara at the age of 22, he had already written his first two books, *Compendium of the Soul* and *Philosophy for the Prosodist*. Some were written in his native language of Persian but most were written in Arabic, the lingua franca of the Muslim world. He was able to recall sources from memory, allowing him to compile works with extensive references to previous scholarship without recourse to these materials.

He had regular periods of literary output. Ibn Sina took a post as a medical attendant at the Persian city of Hamadan and rose to the office of vizier. Every evening he dictated extracts from his works *The Canon* and *The Book of Healing* to his pupils, explaining each principle. Despite his productivity, "only" 200 of his 500 works survive. Many of his books existed as a solitary copy and remained in the libraries of his patrons, which spread from Central Asia to western Iran. Most of those libraries were destroyed in the Mongol onslaught of the 13th and 14th centuries, erasing these books from history.

Ibn Sina's efficacy as a physician in this period is extraordinary considering the limited medieval understanding of human physiology. He was a student of the Roman physician Galen and believed in the four humors. Blood provides vitality, phlegm cools the body, black bile darkens body fluids, and yellow bile aids digestion. Proper health required these humors to remain in balance, leading sometimes to the practice of blood letting.

Despite following the erroneous conventional wisdom of the age, his medical accomplishments are impressive for their time because they were based on hundreds of hours of observation and his powerful deductive logic. Ibn Sina expanded prenatal care, recognized the contagious nature of tuberculosis, and the ability of diseases to spread through impure water. He understood rudimentary psychology, observing connections between physical and emotional states. Ibn Sina even understood the Mozart Effect over 800 years before Mozart himself was born, telling patients to listen to good music to improve their health.

He also provided an accurate description for meningitis, the different parts of the eye and heart valves, and the role of nerves in muscle pain. His integrative approach to the human body opened up new avenues of research for Middle Eastern and European physicians, particularly in the areas of anatomy, gynecology, and pediatrics. His powers of observation extended beyond medicine. In his study of light and optics, Ibn Sina observed the phenomena that light was composed of particles, not waves. Isaac Newton described and Einstein proved this observation centuries later.

Due to his use of deductive logic, Ibn Sina was able to choose productive research paths at a time when many of his fellow scholars went down erroneous academic rabbit trails. He ignored popular but illogical fields of study. Such an approach sounds obvious but is actually quite difficult for a researcher to do in any age. This is due to groupthink and confirmation bias in academia. For example, alchemy was an extremely popular and widely practiced discipline in the Middle Ages. Alchemists believed they were very close to discovering the philosopher's stone, which could turn any sort of base metal such as lead into gold or silver, much as some of today's physicists believe that cold fusion or grand unified theory is around the corner. But Ibn Sina avoided this field altogether, except to write of it in critique. He saved himself years of research in a field that would have born no fruit.

> Art is weaker than nature and does not overtake it, however much it labors. Therefore let the artificers of alchemy know that the species of metals cannot be transmuted. But they can make similar things, and tint a red [metal] with yellow so that it seems gold, and tint a white one with the color that they want until it is very similar to gold or copper. They can also cleanse the impurities of lead, though it will always be lead.

He had a devout belief in logic and rational inquiry because he perceived God as the principle of all existence and pure intellect from whom everything else emanates. Thus physical reality could be grasped and categorized. Ibn Sina believed men improved their lives by improving their intellectual, physical, and spiritual lives; logic, faith, and health lead to a sustained existence. As God was the highest form of intellect, man's quest for human knowledge would draw him closer to God. For this reason his books covered such varying topics as theology and optics. Ibn Sina saw them as the same sort of knowledge, only differing by their material nature.

But Ibn Sina was productive for other reasons than logical deduction. Part of his ability to produce so many written works came from his insatiable drive to research and write, even when he was crippled by poor health. Once on a march of the Isfahan army against Hamadan, he was seized by severe colic so violent that he could not stand. His friends asked him to slow down and avoid such physical strain. He refused, saying "I prefer a short life with width to a narrow one with length." He got his wish: the scholar died at age 58.

Ibn Sina's legacy diminished after his death. His belief in immutable physical laws drew harsh criticism. Al-Ghazali, a 12th-century Muslim scholar whose views came to dominate Islamic scholarship, eviscerated Aristotelian philosophers and all forms of Greek-derived philosophy. Ibn Sina's reputation suffered for the next several centuries in the Middle East because scholarship that favored rational inquiry instead of Islamic holy books fell out of fashion.

But at the same time his reputation rose in Europe. Thirteenth-century German philosopher Albertus Magnus respected him, as did his student Thomas Aquinas, who mentions him on nearly every page of *On Being and Essence*. Ibn Sina's Muslim faith was apparently no problem for these Christian scholars. Bologna professor Girolamo Cardano said that anyone who dismissed Ibn Sina for being a Muslim was a hypocrite for accepting a Roman pagan such as Galen. Venetian physician Genedetto Rinio echoed this idea, pointing out the irony of Renaissance Europe uncritically accepting Roman or Greek natural philosophy while cautiously approaching Muslim scholarship.

Respect for his legacy continues into the modern era. Twentieth-century British philosopher Anthony Few called him "one of the greatest thinkers ever to write in Arabic." Sir William Osler, a Canadian professor of medicine, described him in 1913 as "the author of the most famous medical textbook ever written." They are not exaggerating his accomplishments. Ibn Sina left behind a legacy that subsequent generations explicated and expanded. Critical thinking in medicine, logic, and astronomy spurred new developments. The Middle East and then Europe enjoyed scientific and philosophical golden ages because of his research. In tribute to him there is even a crater on the moon named Avicenna in honor of his contributions to astronomy.

Ibn Sina lived out the principle that the ink of a scholar is more holy than the blood of a martyr. But he could have hardly known the effect that his productive pen would have.

CHAPTER SIXTEEN

THOMAS AQUINAS (1225-1274)

If the family of Thomas Aquinas had any doubt that he was committed to the religious life, their doubts vanished when he chased a prostitute around a room with a firebrand to prevent her from "corrupting" his flesh. They had imprisoned him for two years in the paternal castle of S. Giovanni in order to dissuade him from joining the Dominicans. This newly founded Catholic order demanded an absolute vow of poverty. Thomas was drawn to their emphasis on literacy and learning. His family, however, did not want one of their own to be as poor as a beggar.

In order to rescue him from what they considered to be a religious cult, two of his brothers kidnapped him. According to legend they hired a prostitute and locked her in a room with Thomas for the evening. They hoped he would break his vows of celibacy and be forced to leave the order. Thomas' medieval biographer Bernard Gui describes what happened next: "So a lovely but shameless girl, a very viper in human form, was admitted to the room where Thomas was locked, to corrupt his innocence with wanton words and touches."

Thomas rebuffed her advances in the clearest way possible. He pulled a hot poker from beside the fireplace, fended off her advances and chased her from the room. Thomas then drew a cross on the wall with the smoldering poker and collapsed on the ground, begging for God to grant him the gift of celibacy. The prayer was apparently granted. According to legend, two angels appeared and girded his waist with a cord. It is said that he never struggled with a lustful thought for the rest of his life and became "an angel in the flesh." Gui writes, "From that time onwards, it was his custom to avoid the sight and company of women—except in case of necessity or utility—as a man avoids snakes."

This story illustrates Thomas Aquinas' single-minded focus to his studies, along with his strange social habits (and, what some critics argue, his misogyny). The remarkable output of the medieval theologian is a testimony to his industry. During his lifetime he wrote over 60 tomes of philosophy and theology, most the size of a scholar's magnum opus. The total word count of his extant writings exceeds 6 million words, perhaps the largest set of complete works created by one man before the invention of the word processor. The pages of these books contain dense concepts – much more so than Isaac Asimov's thoughtful-but-workmanlike prose – packing in enough ideas per paragraph to warrant a three-hour graduate student session. They include exegeses of scripture, theological syntheses (Summas), commentaries on church fathers or Aristotelian philosophy, and polemical works. Philosophy professor Peter Kreeft believes that were it not for the scarcity of parchment and ink, Thomas could have written more than 500 books in his lifetime.

Daniel Kennedy wrote of him in the 1912 Catholic Encyclopedia that nobody surpassed him in his economy of words. He synthesized chapters' worth of thoughts in a single paragraph. And he did this in diverse research areas. He wrote in so many different fields that it is impossible to characterize his writing style with one word, unless it is called eclectic. Kennedy's description of Aquinas is worth quoting at length:

> It is Aristotelean, Platonic, and Socratic; it is inductive and deductive; it is analytic and synthetic. He chose the best that he could find in those who preceded him, carefully sifting the chaff from the wheat, approving what was true, rejecting the false. His powers of synthesis were extraordinary. No writer surpassed him in the faculty of expressing in a few well-chosen words the truth gathered from a multitude of varying and conflicting opinions; and in almost every instance the student sees the truth and is perfectly satisfied with St. Thomas' summary and statement.

Thomas' brilliance emerged as a child during his studies at the Benedictine Abbey of Monte Cassino, midway between Rome and Naples. He was described as a witty child who repeatedly posed the question "What is God?" to his tutors. He then spent the next five years in his studies in Naples, where he came in contact with Dominicans and scholars of Aristotle. He studied at the University of Paris, followed by Cologne where he met Albertus Magnus, whose studies on Aristotle strengthened Thomas' own research lines of inquiry. He then returned to Paris, completed his studies at the age of 32, finishing what we would consider to be his doctoral work.

His professional life involved a whirlwind of travel, writing, and debating. Thomas received a three-year appointment to become one of the twelve "masters" in the Faculty of Theology at the University of Paris. He then traveled throughout Italy the following decade to the papal court, Dominican houses, and Rome. He was then called back to Paris to confront the controversy of Latin Averroism, which held that faith and reason were in conflict. This school of thought was an offshoot of an Islamic philosophical branch from 12th-century Muslim scholar Ibn Rushd, who attempted to reconcile Islam with Aristotelianism. After two years in that role, Thomas was assigned to Naples in 1274. While on his way to the Council of Lyon he fell ill. Thomas died in the Cistercian Abbey at Fossanova.

Thomas Aquinas' early writings addressed such issues as the Aristotelian resurgence within mendicant orders. He challenged critics of this movement, such as William of St. Armour, by authoring such works as *Contra impugnantes Dei cultum et religionem* (Against Those Who Assail the Worship of God and Religion). He produced texts on academic and public debates, including *Disputed Questions on Truth* and *Quodlibetal Questions*. Thomas also wrote commentaries on Boethius, a popular philosopher from the sixth century.

Along with these books came commentaries on the gospels *(The Golden Chain* and *Against the Errors of the Greeks)*, written in order to check the influence of ancient Greek philosophy on medieval theology. He wrote on disputes concerning the power of God, which are compiled in his work *De potentia*. He also wrote polemical books such as *On the Eternity of the Word* and *On There Being Only One Intellect*. Following these books came the completion of the *Summa Theologica* – his largest and most influential work. It is a cyclical historical overview of the cosmos and its ultimate purpose, beginning with God. He demonstrates God's existence with five proofs, using Aristotle's argument of the unmoved mover. Other sections include Creation, Man, Man's Purpose, Christ, and the Sacraments.

Much of the reason that Aquinas wrote such a massive body of literature was in order to sway academic opinion on a complex and controversial issue. In the 1200s, the theological controversy of the time was the connection between reason and faith. Aquinas believed that these worked in collaboration. Faith guided reason and could prevent it from falling into error, while reason could demystify faith. He argued that the existence of God could be proved by identifying

God as the cause of everything. Varying levels of human perfection necessitated the existence of a supreme, perfect being.

During his stint as the regent master at the University of Paris from 1268 to 1272, he refuted those following the philosophy of Aristotle to deny such Christian doctrines as the creation of the universe and the immortality of the soul. Those that held this position followed the scholarship of Ibn Rushd and put reason against faith. Aquinas argued in contrast that correct reason never contradicted true faith. Ibn Rushd's philosophy held that reason conflicted with the doctrine of Christ's union between man and God. Thomas said this mistaken understanding of Aristotle's philosophy wrongly introduced a separation between philosophy and theology.

It was no easy task for Aquinas to convince scholars that Aristotle – the greatest and most prolific philosopher of ancient Greece – could be reconciled with Christianity. Integrating Aristotelian philosophy and Christian theology, two fields with centuries of scholarship, would be a work of dozens of theologians. Aquinas decided to do it by himself. His summaries of Aristotle include *On Being and Essence* and *The Principles of Nature*. His commentary on Aristotle *On the Soul* is only one of 11 Aristotelian works.

Among all his writings, Thomas' greatest work is the *Summa Theologica* (The Summation of Theology). The title is no exaggeration. It is over 2 million words long, a work of systematic philosophy and theology as massive as the Great Pyramid of Giza. He integrated Biblical theology, Aristotle, Augustine, Jerome, and other church fathers; the Jewish philosopher Maimonides; Muslim scholars Ibn Sina and Ibn Rushd; and other figures popular in medieval philosophy. No other work of scholarship has been as influential in the history of Christianity. It systemized theology as no one had done before. The *Summa* remains required reading for any Christian theologian. It had such a large influence on Dante

Alighieri's *Divine Comedy* that the epic poem has been called "the *Summa* in verse."

Aquinas was able to achieve such a high level of writing output due to a number of factors. Not the least was his extraordinary mental powers. According to Saint Antonius, Aquinas "remembered everything he had read, so that his mind was like a huge library." To this praise Aquinas humbly agreed. He noted that the greatest grace he had ever received was to understand whatever he had read. That is not to say that he was always considered brilliant. During his studies with Albertus Magnus, his classmates called him a "dumb ox" – perhaps for his quiet disposition and enormous girth. One day Albertus invited Thomas to explain a difficult philosophical text. His lucid explanation stunned the class, prompting Albertus to predict that soon the entire world would hear "the bellowing of this dumb ox..."

Other legends of his extraordinary focus filter down through church biographies and hagiographies. One day a fellow student joked with him and tried to rouse him out of his studies. He said, "Brother Thomas, look at this ox flying!" Thomas walked to the window, and when others burst out laughing at him, he replied, "I should be less surprised to see an ox flying, than to find a religious [brother] lying."

Thomas spoke rarely and never without good cause. At social events he mingled little with others, likely caught up with an intellectual quandary. When he did emerge from his monastic cell and take a break from his writing, Thomas walked alone along the cloisters at great speed, head up and uncovered. He rarely went out and often refused invitations from aristocrats or royalty, only attending when under obedience. Thomas considered few things important outside of his studies. Once when returning from Saint-Denis and seeing before him the whole city of Paris, his travel companion asked if he would not like to possess the whole city. He replied that he would rather have a certain manuscript from John Chrysostom that he lacked.

According to one episode in his life Thomas attended a dinner hosted by St. Louis, the king of France. Thomas ignored the conversation of the esteemed company and instead focused on a polemic against the Manicheans, a Persian religion that synthesized Zoroastrian dualism, gnosticism, and Buddhist ethics. He then erupted from his silence and startled the crowd by pounding on the table and shouting, "That settles the Manicheans!" Louis apparently knew of the scholar's quirks and called for a secretary to record his thoughts. Another story relates that a scribe dictated the words of Thomas, who was so deep in thought that a candle burned his hand without the scholar noticing.

As a Dominican friar, Thomas lived a far more structured life than most people in the Middle Ages. Here is a breakdown of his daily schedule, according to biographer Bartholomew of Capua. It explains how Thomas did more in his 30 years as a scholar (Aquinas died at age of 49) than most could do in a century:

1.He celebrated Mass early in the morning.

2.He stayed in chapel to attend a second Mass celebrated by another priest.

3.Then he went to teach.

4.After that, he began to write and would dictate to his secretaries, sometimes to three or even four at the same time.

5.Only then did he go to eat.

6.Then he went back to his room where he "attended to divine things" until rest. After rest, began again to write.

This schedule does not begin to delve into the busyness of his life. Aquinas lived in a friary and had to follow daily practices of common prayer, Eucharistic celebrations, and community meetings. Added to these were hours of daily personal prayer and meditation. He often went to the chapel in the middle of the night to pray alone, then returned to his cell before morning prayers when he prayed again with his brothers. He followed a precise schedule of writing, teaching, prayer, contemplation, and eating. And he did eat. Thomas was famous for his large size; a crescent was cut out of a dinner table to accommodate his girth. G.K. Chesterton described him as "the sort of walking wine-barrel, common in the comedies of many nations."

Beyond his regimented schedule, Aquinas was able to achieve a prolific writing output because he could detach himself from intellectual arguments and avoid inserting himself into unnecessary debates. This is remarkable in an age when intellectuals resorted to petty insults and even violence against one another. When he took an appointment at the University of Paris, he had to attend his first lecture with an armed guard because the presence of Dominicans on the faculty was viciously opposed by other masters. Despite the heated nature of the debate, Thomas maintained incredible self-control in his controversies. He appeared rarely annoyed by a contradiction. John Peckham was among his most vocal critics, but even he admitted that after an interview in which he attacked Thomas with vehemence, he replied "with rare gentleness and humility."

Not answering each and every critic also saved Thomas time by focusing on his own writings, not wasting his time on squabbles that would divert attention from research. Even though he had an intellect that could act, as Chesterton says, "like a huge system of artillery spread over the whole world," he only used his wits to defend truths distinct from himself. He had what historians describe as an "intellectual unconsciousness," even an intellectual innocence. His writings appear completely impartial. Due to his mental discipline, Thomas hides his personality in his works, as his opinions are removed from the simple clarity of his language. Other great writers inserted their own writing style or flair into their works; Thomas sharpened his thoughts to such a fine point that he removes it completely. This explains why his writings have persisted throughout the centuries. Thomas engaged with timeless moral questions that are of interest to today's students of philosophy or theology. Had he spent his time in disputes with other authors, his polemics would have been so bound to the political climate of the 13th century that they would be unintelligible to anyone but medieval scholars.

Despite his extraordinary mental abilities, Aquinas was able to remain productive through the powers of delegation. He trusted those around him to do the tasks that he could not do himself or did not have the time to do. For example, he had terrible penmanship. Extant writing samples of his are famously illegible. To compensate, he developed an elaborate system of dictation. It resembled a chess grandmaster at a simultaneous exhibition, playing multiple challengers all at once. Thomas delegated his writing to scribes by standing in the center of a circle of five scribes at five desks. He turned to the first, recited two or three lines of whatever work project at the time, such as *Aristotle's Metaphysics*. He then went to the second scribe, who was perhaps recording a Bible commentary, and gave him two or three more lines. Thomas turned to the third scribe, giving him a few lines on a commentary of Boethius' book on the Trinity. He gave a few more sentences to the fourth and fifth scribes on other projects, whether a personal letter to the pope or course lecture notes. He continued around the circle like this for hours.

Above all, Thomas' great productivity can be explained by his understanding of his own purpose in life. He maintained direction in his work by grasping the common intention behind each of his books, paragraphs, and sentences. He knew his *teleology* – the final destiny and goal of his life. He tells us his teleology in the introduction of the *Summa Theologica*. Aquinas says that the purpose of a man is not to be rich, married, or healthy, but to be happy in God with the Beatific vision. The book is concerned with goals, or final causality. All other daily, weekly, monthly, and yearly goals can be subordinated to this larger purpose.

This purpose was explicit in Thomas' thinking, so much so that according to legend a year before his death he had a vision of the crucified Christ. He spoke to Aquinas, saying, "You have written well of me, Thomas. What would you ask of me?" To which Thomas replied, "Nothing else but you, Lord." Compared to what he had seen from this experience, Thomas replied that everything he had written seemed of no more value than straw. He never took up his pen to write theology again.

This story encapsulates Thomas' life as a scholar. He did not write scholarship for scholarship's sake. He saw it as a path to a destination. He considered his theological and philosophical studies as a means to an end of his teleology: attaining greater understanding of God. Aquinas reminded himself of this task each day by repeating a simple prayer before he began his studies. This prayer has become famous among theologians and seminarians, who similarly repeat it to gain clarity of mind before sitting down to study, reading a difficult text, or writing on a thorny intellectual topic.

Creator of all things, true source of light and wisdom, origin of all being, graciously let a ray of your light penetrate the darkness of my understanding.
Take from me the double darkness in which I have been born, an obscurity of sin and ignorance.

Give me a keen understanding, a retentive memory, and the ability to grasp things correctly and fundamentally
Grant me the talent of being exact in my explanations and the ability to express myself with thoroughness and charm.
Point out the beginning, direct the progress, and help in the completion. I ask this through Jesus Christ our Lord. Amen.

Historians of Thomas Aquinas – whether or not they are religious – cannot argue that this prayer was granted. The Catholic Church embraced the scholarship of Thomas as official teachings of the church. It still fully endorses his writings 800 years after his death. His clarity of writing and powerful arguments conquered his intellectual opponents. Thomas' productivity allowed him to answer many foes and integrate Christianity with Aristotelian philosophy. He did all these things before his 50th birthday.

Not bad for a dumb ox.

CHAPTER SEVENTEEN

CATHERINE OF SIENA (1347-1380)

Catherine of Siena had an atypical upbringing for a theologian, mystic, and Italian diplomat. She was the 23rd child of a poor family and unable to write until three years before her death at 33. She spent years as a low-ranking member of a religious order and primarily spent her days in solitude and prayer. One of her few responsibilities was to tend to the sick as the Black Death ravaged Europe.

But by the end of her life Catherine had traveled throughout the Italian peninsula as a diplomat and negotiated peace between princes. She wrote dozens of letters to Pope Gregory and convinced him to restore the papacy in Rome. She authored "The Dialogue," a treatise on a fictional conversation between a saint and God, which influenced theologians and the lay religious for centuries. She was named a joint Patron Saint of Italy along with Francis of Assisi in 1939 and a Doctor of the Church by Pope Paul VI in 1970. While stories about her life are filled with miracles and very much hagiographic, they depicted a woman who managed to wield enormous power in the most unlikely of ways.

Catherine was born in 1347 to Jacopo Benincasa, a wool dyer, and Japa Benincasa, the daughter of a poet. She had a joyful disposition from her early years, and her family gave her the nickname Euphrosyne: Greek for "joy" and the name of an early Christian saint. She grew up during a time of enormous social upheaval in Europe. Following a century of commercial growth, the Black Plague began ravaging the continent in the 1340s. Disease, hunger, and death depleted the population. Feudal lords insisted that peasants continued paying high taxes, but they sensed that officials had little means to punish them. Rebellion formed in rural areas. The urban poor also rose up in protest against the upper classes, who used their political power to keep wages low. The papacy was caught up in this turmoil, falling under control of the French crown.

Catherine was said by her confessor and biographer Raymond of Capua to have seen her first vision of Christ at the age of 6. In this vision he was adorned as a pope, seated on a throne, and surrounded by Peter, Paul, and John, all of whom appeared in the sky over the church of San Domenico. Catherine's brother Stephen saw her stand with an entranced look on her face; he had to seize her by the hand to wake her from the dream-like state. Catherine burst into tears afterwards and made a vow the following year to devote herself to God, forsaking marriage.

Her desire to serve in the church brought her into conflict with her family, who sought to marry her off. When she was 12 her mother urged her to mind her appearance in order to enter a marriage arrangement. Four years later her parents pressured her to marry the widower of her sister Bonaventura, who had died in childbirth. Catherine refused to do so and fasted until her parents capitulated. She cut off her long, brown hair in defiance of her mother's wishes and repented of any form of vanity.

To punish her, Japa tasked Catherine with managing the household. With her large number of brothers and sisters, this was certainly backbreaking labor. The responsibility always kept her in the presence of others, perhaps the worst of all punishments for the solitude-craving girl. This episode was critical in the development of her monastic approach to prayer. In *The Dialogue*, she wrote that this period in her life taught her how to build in her soul "a private cell where no tribulation could enter."

Catherine dedicated herself to the church that year. She joined the Dominican Tertiaries, an organization of the faithful who lived their lives according to a religious order but did not take religious vows. The members of the order protested her application and questioned her motivation, since a typical female tertiary was widowed or elderly. They finally accepted Catherine, likely as a result of her mother's pleading, who feared her daughter would starve herself to death through fasting if denied service to the church. She became an anchoress, a person who had retired from the world in prayer, and spent her days beseeching God in a small room in her father's house.

Paradoxically, Catherine gained opportunities for social advancement as an anchoress. It gave a woman considerable influence in a medieval community, even if most of her days were spent alone and she rarely ventured outside except to celebrate Mass. If a cobbler or local magistrate had theological questions or simply needed practical advice, he would often seek out an anchoress. She was considered to have unique communication with God and able to offer divine insight. Since she was in contact with various members of the community, an anchoress could also be a good source of news, a person's whereabouts, and especially gossip. Her advice was even sought out by local politicians.

Catherine's early anchoress years, in which she acted as the town's unofficial psychologist and consultant, proved essential in the coming decades when she moved up from the local level to the regional and international levels. She also took advantage of educational opportunities that the Catholic Church offered women in the 14th century. Through the Dominican order she learned to read. She also acquired knowledge of Greek and Latin. She engaged in theological discourse with her confessor, an informal type of religious training that likely equipped her to write *The Dialogue* years later.

Catherine only left her tiny cell to attend Mass and spoke to few others besides her confessor. She broke up sessions of contemplative prayer with acts of self-mortification that were common in medieval holy orders. Such acts included scourging herself with an iron chain three times a day or sleeping on a board as a means to embrace poverty. She claimed in this period to have had celestial visitations and conversations with Christ.

In 1368 the 21-year-old underwent an earth-shattering experience that caused her to abandon her life of solitude and enter public life. According to *The Dialogue* she experienced what she interpreted in her letters as a "Mystical Marriage with Jesus." This is an event that Catholic mystics describe as a deep spiritual union between the devout and Christ, in which the former is deemed worthy to participate in the latter's sufferings so that others may be blessed.

It is "the accompaniment and symbol of a purely spiritual grace," and "that as a wife should share in the life of her husband, and as Christ suffered for the redemption of mankind, the mystical spouse enters into a more intimate participation in His sufferings." In the vision, Christ gave Catherine a gold ring with four precious stones and a diamond in the middle to symbolize their spiritual union. She wrote that it always remained visible to her but invisible to others.

Catherine was now prepared to offer herself sacrificially to the world. She rejoined her family and used the household as a base to tend to the sick and poor of Siena, an enormous effort at the height of the Black Death. Such labors involved burying plague victims, a lowly and dangerous task that she often did herself, much as Francis of Assisi had done for lepers. "Never did she appear more admirable than at this time," wrote a priest who had known her from girlhood. "She was always with the plague-stricken; she prepared them for death and buried them with her own hands. I myself witnessed the joy with which she nursed them and the wonderful efficacy of her words, which brought about many conversions." This stage of Catherine's ministry inspired other Catholic humanitarians in the following centuries, particularly Mother Teresa and her mission to the poor in Calcutta.

Catherine gave food and clothing to anyone in need. She volunteered to nurse the ill in hospitals. She visited criminals in Siena's prison. These pious actions caused men and women to gather around her, which Catherine described as a spiritual fellowship bound by mystical bonds of love. Some in Siena regarded her as a saint while others considered her a fanatic.

As her popularity grew, she was summoned to Florence to appear before the general chapter of the Dominicans to determine if her teachings were orthodox. In the late medieval period the Catholic Church carefully watched the development of religious movements for fear of a heresy spreading or a radical religious movement threatening its relationship with European monarchs. She was found to possess right teaching. Raymond de Capua was appointed her confessor. He also acted as her disciple and biographer.

Catherine and her followers first sought social reform in Italy. At this time the peninsula was massively corrupt and mired in warfare. Church offices were frequently bought and sold. Cardinals split into political factions based on which European monarch provided them the most financial support. The granting of indulgences, in which the Church offered the remission of temporal sin in exchange for a considerable donation, became so widespread that it became the financial means by which the Catholic Church launched military campaigns.

The papacy was so poisoned by politics that it inspired Machiavelli to write *The Prince* 150 years later. It attempted to play the city-states of Venice, Florence, Milan, and Naples against one another to consolidate its military strength against the Holy Roman Emperor, but could not create a balance of power. Warfare in Italy was rooted in the conflict between the Papal States and the Tuscan states and its allies. The French crown made a move during this disorder and relocated the papacy to Avignon, France in 1307. Italian leagues formed against the pope to return it to Rome and defy the Avignon Papacy, which was later referred to as the "Babylonian Captivity of the Papacy." The church increasingly fell under the influence of the French crown.

Catherine was convicted to clear out this snake pit. Her consulting abilities acquired as an anchoress in Siena were put to the test, albeit on a much larger scale. She sent letters to the princes of Italy, rebuking them for politicking and corruption. Most politicians would have likely crumpled up and thrown away such a letter from a lowly church member, but her movement already had power. She was beloved by the lay population, and those in high positions knew it. Due to her growing profile as a political intermediary, she was consulted by papal legates about the affairs of the church.

Catherine had scribes write hundreds of letters to clerics, magistrates, and leaders of Italy's city-states to negotiate peace. Her chief aim was to return the papacy from Avignon to Rome. The uneducated tertiary even began writing to Pope Gregory XI in what turned into a long correspondence. She referred to him affectionately as "papa" (pope) rather than the ceremonial "Your Holiness," kindly, but firmly, urging him to return to Italy. There is question as to how much influence Catherine had on the outcome of the papacy's return to Rome. Whatever degree it was, she was not someone to be ignored at this time, whether in theological or diplomatic circles.

Papal legates sent her on a diplomatic mission in 1375 after war broke out between Florence, the Holy See, and the French legates. Two powerful Florentine factions united to create a large army and gain independence from the pope's control. She was sent to sway Pisa and Lucca into neutrality and away from an alliance with the anti-papal league. Catherine was one of the few figures that was trusted and respected on all sides. Although she was an ardent defender of the pope, Florence sent her as diplomat to Avignon to make peace. The mission failed, but she made an impression on Pope Gregory, who decided to return to Rome despite the protests of the College of Cardinals and the French king.

In 1378 he sent her to Florence to formalize a peace accord between it and the Holy See. These diplomatic missions put Catherine in considerable danger, as opposing factions often made attempts on her life. This resulted from the anchoress becoming a polarizing figure in Italy. Some historians believe that Catherine was used as a pawn by the papal legates against other city-states, in particular by her confessor Raymond. There is plausibility to this argument, as all of her correspondence supporting the papal line occurs after 1374, after she was summoned to the general chapter of the Dominican Order.

Catherine returned to Rome to assist the papacy during the outbreak of the Western Schism, a split between the Church from 1378 to 1417. After Gregory's death the cardinals elected Urban VI, who proved to be highly unpopular and ill-suited to the post. The majority of the cardinals regretted their decision and elected Robert of Geneva, even though Urban was still ruling. Robert established his court back in Avignon, becoming Antipope Clement VII. There was now a pope and anti-pope set up by the same group. France, Spain, Scotland and Naples recognized Clement. Urban was recognized by North Italy, England, Flanders, and Hungary.

Catherine fiercely advocated for Urban VI against the newly restored French line. Yet the 31-year-old also counseled him that he needed to learn to control his sharp and angry temper. The scolded pontiff was not only obedient, but he sent for Catherine from Siena that she might come to Rome and counsel him. The request is not as strange as it sounds. She was widely sought after for her wisdom by other high-ranking church officials, including theologians from Siena, Avignon, and Genoa.

As an advisor to Europe's church factions, Catherine held significant political power but she was first and foremost a tertiary and mystic. Ironically, it was her religious conviction that led to her undoing. Catherine's penchant for fasting began to consume her. She ate less and less over the years, sometimes subsisting for months on nothing but the Eucharist. Raymond ordered her to eat, but Catherine claimed that she was simply unable to do so. On April 21, 1380 she suffered a paralytic stroke and lost any sensation from the waist down. Eight days later she died at the age of 33.

Her religious legacy grew quickly after her death. Dying young at the peak of one's fame created a mythology around Catherine's life, much as it did other religious figures such as Joan of Arc or Jan de Bakker. Fellow Italians compared her writings to those of Dante Alighieri. Parts of her body were enshrined in St. Dominic's Church as a holy relic. It soon became a popular pilgrimage site. In the centuries since then, Catherine has cast a towering influence in Catholic theology.

Her most famous work is *The Dialogue*, which analyzes the entire spiritual life of man in the form of conversations between God and a human interlocutor, as represented by Catherine. It is written in the simple but beautiful Tuscan Italian of the 14th century and has been a classic work of spiritual contemplation for centuries.

In her other writings she is honest concerning the difficulties of life as a Christian mystic. Her visions were not always pleasant encounters with Christ or the saints. She was besieged by terrible temptations and loathsome forms. At brief times, these caused her to believe that she had been forsaken by God. Yet she always recovered. Miraculous signs abounded in her life. Her biographer wrote that in 1375 she received the stigmata, or visible signs of the marks of Christ.

Today, Catherine is beloved for kindness to people from all levels of society, whether popes or criminals. In 1375 she assisted the political prisoner, Niccolo di Tuldo, at his execution. She actively sought out plague victims when others walled them off to die in solitude for fear of contracting the mysterious illness. For this reason she is the namesake of many Catholic hospitals today.

And yet Catherine would likely not consider such deeds as the most important feather in her cap. The Italian theologian considered the sentiments behind the action far more important than the action itself. If something was not done for love, then it was not worth doing. In a famous line from *The Dialogue*, she related this concept in her characteristic succinct style: "You are rewarded not according to your work or your time, but according to the measure of your love."

CHAPTER EIGHTEEN

CHARLES SPURGEON (1834-1892)

Charles Spurgeon was a Victorian-era Baptist preacher who led the Metropolitan Tabernacle for 38 years. By the time of his death in 1892 at the age of 57, he had preached to an estimated 10 million people. His sermons were published weekly by his church's press, selling more than 100 million copies in 23 languages by the end of the 19th century, making him the most published preacher of all time. He also wrote 135 books, including poetry, hymns, devotionals, Bible commentaries, and an autobiography. Over a century after his death, his literature is still widely circulated in Christian circles, totaling over 300 million copies. He retains the title "The Prince of Preachers."

But it is his other work habits that astound people today, whether or not they work in a religious vocation. His weekly schedule was busier than a Wall Street stockbroker's. He prepared numerous sermons, edited a magazine, launched multiple charities connected to his church, established a pastor's college named

Spurgeon's College – where he lectured weekly – and founded the Stockwell Orphanage in 1867. By accepting so many invitations from other churches to speak, he often preached up to 10 times in a week.

He was matter-of-fact about all these responsibilities. Spurgeon remarked in his autobiography: "No one living knows the toil and care I have to bear. I ask for no sympathy but ask indulgence if I sometimes forget something. I have to look after the Orphanage, have charge of a church with four thousand members, sometimes there are marriages and burials to be undertaken, there is the weekly sermon to be revised, "The Sword and the Trowel" to be edited, and besides all that, a weekly average of five hundred letters to be answered."

Spurgeon was born in 1834 in a small village in England. His father and grandfather were both pastors. He embraced Christianity at age 15 on a snowy day in January at a Methodist church, when a visiting pastor called on him to "look unto Christ." He undertook self-study of theology. At age 17, he was ordained a pastor at Waterbeach Baptist Church, located near Cambridge. Spurgeon then took a post at New Park Street Baptist Church in the south of London, later renamed Metropolitan Tabernacle, where he remained for 38 years.

His ministry in London soon exploded. When Spurgeon began there were only 200 attendees, who shuffled into a building that should have seated over 1,200. It was a dingy environment and the congregation was in decline. The fiery young pastor changed that. He preached in a plain but old-fashioned Puritan style, in contrast to the high-church eloquence of Anglican clergy. Attendance soon jumped into the thousands. He was soon a media sensation, with London reporters curious about his meteoric rise. Press attacks on his preaching style soon followed. Another minister predicted that he would rise like a firework, explode, but quickly fall back to earth.

Spurgeon became famous for his preaching abilities, but he stayed influential for decades by building a highly effective publishing infrastructure. His greatest innovation as a preacher was his method of syndicating content. Spurgeon could take a simple sermon outline and have it turned into published sermon notes, books, pamphlets, and other literature for England's religious class. This publishing system was nearly a century ahead of its time. It would not be until the late 20th century, when self-help gurus like Tony Robbins were able to replicate his success of taking one piece of content and turning it into multiple products, spinning off a 5-day self-help conference into a book, DVD set, or online course.

This was Spurgeon's method for accomplishing so much with so little time. He found the small, effective habits that were most beneficial to his ministry. He then systematized them, handed off the tasks to others, automated them, then watched his efforts compound. His church media would flow out from his parish and spread throughout London, then England, then the rest of the world. "The way to do a great deal is to keep on doing a little," he said. "The way to do nothing at all is to be continually resolving that you will do everything."

The seeds for his publishing empire were his sermon notes. Creating them required a few days of study and consulting Bible commentaries. He also read five or six Christian scholarly books of considerable length per week. Spurgeon had a powerful mind and could read nearly a page a second, usually finishing a book in one setting. Over his lifetime he read more than 12,000 books, which he kept in his personal library.

Then came time to preach. Two stenographers transcribed his Sunday sermon as he spoke. On Monday or Tuesday he edited the sermon transcript for publication. The press then printed off at least 25,000 copies, which sold for a penny each. This number may seem small, but he sold this many copies each week for four decades. His church produced more than 50 million copies of his sermons by the time of his death. In the following decades the number swelled to nearly 300 million copies in 41 languages.

His publishing efforts went outside of his sermons. He released the monthly magazine *The Sword and the Trowel*. He also wrote a seven-volume commentary on the Psalms in 1885 called *The Treasury of David*. In the book he analyzed each verse in the similar way that he preached – spending pages on a single verse, drawing in themes and stories from the most obscure corners of the Bible, weaving together a complex theological tapestry. The pastor also took his talents outside of the church. He preached nearly every day at different churches in London or at local parishes in the countryside. Spurgeon also guest lectured at The Pastor's College. He composed addresses titled *Lectures to My Students* that were a publishing success in their own right.

Spurgeon's amount of output cannot be completely credited to a complex productivity system – although he did utilize the help of those around him whenever he could. Spurgeon used stenographers to answer the letters that flooded his office. With the help of two secretaries he dictated and answered over 500 letters per week.

Most of all, his productivity is attributed to what he would describe as a holy calling, but what the secular realm would describe as sheer workaholism. The preacher acknowledged that his efforts went beyond his abilities and taxed his health. But he took pride in his exertions, considering them a sacrifice in order to build God's kingdom. To his students at The Pastor's College he wrote that, "We are all too much occupied with taking care of ourselves. We shun the difficulties of excessive labour." Spurgeon made good on this statement. He often worked 18 hours a day. When missionary and explorer of Africa David Livingstone asked him how he managed to do the work of two men in a single day, he responded, "It is not I who do it." Here Spurgeon was paraphrasing Philippians 2:13, which said, "For it is God who works in you, both to will and to work for His good pleasure."

A chapter in his autobiography entitled "A Typical Week's Work" details his schedule, which is enough to produce work-related stress merely by reading it. Even though Spurgeon was famous for his sermons, he could not actually sit down and begin writing them until Saturday evening because the rest of his week was completely filled with other duties. He could only mentally record bits and scraps of information throughout the week that he would compile the night before he was supposed to enter the pulpit and preach in front of thousands.

On Sunday, Spurgeon arrived at the church half an hour before the service began. He selected the hymns that were to be sung and arranged the music best adapted to them. He began preaching promptly at 11 o'clock and continued for nearly two hours to what the London media described as "a spellbound audience." After concluding, there was usually a long procession of parishioners and guests from foreign lands who waited to shake his hand and greet the pastor. Dozens of ministers usually attended a Sunday sermon, with many traveling all the way from America to England by steamer, hoping to secure a private interview with the celebrity pastor. Spurgeon had an uncanny ability to remember names and faces, even if they had only met once years before. This meet-and-greet period continued until 4 pm, when Spurgeon would get an hour of rest before the evening service.

On Monday he began revising the sermon transcript that his stenographers recorded. This was an important task for Spurgeon, who knew that to delay the publication even for a week would hurt circulation numbers. As Spurgeon revised the sermon on Monday, his private secretary J.W. Harrald opened the morning's letters and arrange those that required immediate answers. The secretary threw away anonymous letters that were excessively negative – or even abusive – in order not to unnecessarily distract Spurgeon. The pastor occasionally dictated replies to letters before continuing his sermon revising, sometimes writing a response himself. This became necessary in later years when donations increased, as a generous donor could not be ignored or "dismissed" by a dictated letter. He finished revising the sermon by the end of Monday, then began answering letters, reviewing books, proofing magazine articles, or tending to other literary works.

He then met with numerous callers. Often times those who came sought Spurgeon because he always issued an open invitation in his Sunday sermons that anyone who was moved to seek an interest in Christ meet with him at his vestry on Monday morning. After holding a few dozen of these meetings, Spurgeon – if he had a break at all – spent a few minutes strolling outside before returning to his work.

He then went straight to the Tabernacle at 5:30 pm either to meet with the church elders or preside at the first part of a church meeting, often to greet new members. Spurgeon chaired the meeting until 7 pm, then handed it off to his brother, and left to preside over a prayer meeting. He never missed this meeting if he could help it, as he considered it the thermometer of the church's health. The meeting finished at 8:30 pm.

But Spurgeon's day was not finished. Many visitors waited for an interview with him after the prayer meeting if he lingered about. Sometimes he left promptly after it finished to preach at another congregation on behalf of a benevolent fund.

Then Tuesday began. Spurgeon checked over the sermon proof again, completing it by 11 o'clock, leaving a couple of hours to reply to more letters. In the afternoon he met candidates for church membership at the Tabernacle – and Spurgeon met *personally* with every one of the thousands of people who sought membership. For the next three or four hours he met with between 20 and 40 candidates. At 5 pm he had a brief tea break and compared notes with his helpers for half an hour concerning those with whom he had conversed. He then returned to his task of meeting with candidates and continued for as long as there were still people waiting. Once finished, he went down to the lecture hall to preside over an annual meeting of one of the many Tabernacle societies – these included the Sunday School, the Almshouse Day School, the Evangelists' Association, the Country Mission, the Loan Tract Society, or the Spurgeon's Sermons' Tract Society. There were so many different societies attached to the church that it would have been possible to have an anniversary of one of them every week of the year. At these meetings there were between hundreds and thousands of attendees.

On Wednesday he took a mid-week Sabbath rest. Spurgeon told his secretary to keep his schedule clear of all appointments that day. This was a good idea in theory, but it rarely worked in practice. Appointments sprung up and demanded attention; the pastor rarely had the heart to refuse them. Although Spurgeon did his best to turn them down, knowing that the result of too much work would be a breakdown in health, he kept up these appointments until his health actually did break down and he started following through on his Sabbath Wednesday. But as soon as Spurgeon recovered, he inevitably turned his vacation day back into a work day. Requests for sermons, speeches, and lectures flooded in even during his worst illnesses. He rarely refused.

Thursday was devoted to letter writing. Since Spurgeon's sermons had spread across the world, his fans were distributed globally. He spent so much time in return correspondence that he lamented in his autobiography, "I am only a poor clerk, driving the pen hour after hour; here is another whole morning gone, and nothing done but letters, letters, letters!" Although it was sheer drudgery, the pastor considered this work part of his ministry. He believed a response from him could comfort a troubled heart. When this business was finished, he retired to his summer house and his garden and worked on his commentary of Psalms or some of his other books.

After dinner, he began preparations for the Thursday evening service, preaching on a topic that had been "simmering" in his mind all morning. A secretary would research anything that might help him get the true meaning of a scriptural text, which reduced the time necessary to prepare a sermon. From 6 to 7 pm, Spurgeon hosted an extra gathering in the Tabernacle lecture hall called "The Pastor's Prayer-Meeting." It was convened for the purpose of seeking a blessing on the Sunday sermon. Many Christian workers from all denominations who were not able to be present on Sunday attended this meeting, among them many Anglican clergy. Many of those who attended sought an audience with Spurgeon at the end of the meeting, so it was very late before he finished the day.

On Friday he prepared a talk for the students of the Pastor's College. This preparatory effort went on for hours until he gave his lecture in the afternoon. Spurgeon perhaps exerted more efforts on this talk than anything else, save his Sunday sermon, as he considered the training of the next generation of pastors a critical work. He lectured from 3 to 5 pm. Many students said that of all his preaching and teaching, Spurgeon's most brilliant utterances were in those lectures. After it finished, he met with students for the next hour.

Sometimes Spurgeon returned home, but more often he attended some other anniversary meeting or presided over an evening class connected with the College. Other times there was a sick or dying member of the church to whom he had sent word that he would call on his way back from the College. Although there were too many church members for him to visit personally, he met with as many as he could. His sermons include many references to deathbed scenes that he had witnessed. He also conducted funerals and weddings when time permitted.

His wife wrote in Spurgeon's biography that with all of these weekly responsibilities, "add to all this, the constant interruptions from callers, and the many minor worries to which every public man is subject, and readers may well wonder when Spurgeon could find time for reading, and study, and all the work he constantly accomplished! If they had known how much he was continually doing, they might have marveled even more than they did. Surely, there never was a busier life than his; not an atom more of sacred service could have been crowded into it."

The sheer amount of work that Spurgeon undertook caused him significant health problems. From 35 onward he suffered gout. This condition reduced him to a bedridden state for weeks or even months at a time. Beginning in the 1870s, he showed symptoms of Bright's disease, which is chronic inflammation of the kidneys. He also suffered rheumatism. All of these conditions were exacerbated by his frequent cigar smoking, which he embraced with no moderation or apology. When a parishioner asked him how much smoking was too much, he responded, "More than one cigar at a time."

He was perhaps more plagued by the controversies of his ministry than his workload. Spurgeon's insouciant preaching style and popularity earned him enemies in England's religious establishment. He was an object of scorn among London's elite social classes. The controversy, which took the worst toll on him, and may have led to his early death, was the Downgrade Controversy. The Baptist Union, an umbrella organization to which Spurgeon's church was a member, began accepting members who held higher critical views of Scripture, such as denying the substitutionary atonement or accepting the theory of evolution – a great controversy in 19th century conservative Christian circles. Spurgeon withdrew from the Baptist Union, which responded by formally censoring him.

Despite his massive workload and health problems, Spurgeon refused to slow down. He considered himself tasked with the same responsibilities as St. Paul, who through his physical suffering demonstrated the physical humility of Christ to those around him.

During his first significant illness in 1858 he wrote to his congregation and readers: "Do not attribute this illness to my having laboured too hard for my Master. For his dear sake, I would that I may yet be able to labour more." Later, in a sermon, he stated: "I look with pity upon people who say 'Do not preach so often; you will kill yourself.' O my God! what would Paul have said to such a thing as that?"

Aside from his workaholism, the lessons of Spurgeon's productivity are applicable to the religious and secular alike. He multiplied his effectiveness by handing off tasks to those around him. He maintained a clear schedule. He had large goals in mind, and this vision helped him overcome day-to-day difficulties.

There are also negative lessons to draw from his life. No rest or recreation can cause severe health problems, actually producing a net loss in productivity. Workaholism is ultimately destructive, no matter how it is dressed up for higher purposes. But in taking these lessons together – both positive and negative – the examples of Spurgeon's life are useful for anyone seeking greater effectiveness.

CONCLUSION

PRODUCTIVE LIVING IN 21ST-CENTURY OFFICE CUBICLE CULTURE

Benjamin Franklin or Theodore Roosevelt would do poorly in a 21st century office job. With their results-driven approach to work, they would skip meetings and ignore their manager's 2-hour presentations. Their boss would consider them lacking dedication for not listening to ambiguous executive nonsense. But while he droned on, they would likely find ways to boost company profits several times over. Roosevelt would secure a $3 million order by challenging a client to a sparring duel if he refused. Franklin would run to his print shop, launch a pamphlet advertising campaign, and boost company profits by 70 percent. But their manager would quickly tire of these antics, no matter the results. He would fire them, preferring more compliant office drones who quietly put in 10-hour days and accomplish very little by comparison.

The scenario is hypothetical, but managerial preference for non-productive but compliant workers is a fact. According to a 2010 study published in *Human Relations*, bosses judge their employees according to how many hours they log in each day, regardless of what they do with those hours. In the study, a research team led by business professor Kimberly Elsbach interviewed 39 corporate managers. They found that managers considered those employees who spent more hours in the office to be more hardworking, dedicated, and responsible. Never mind that even if an employee found ways to complete their work ahead of their slower colleagues, they were still judged as less hardworking than their office mates.

Elsbach references the story of an employee named Chris who managed to get all his work done during the week and did not need to put in overtime. But the manager preferred other team members for coming in on Saturdays. He faulted Chris, who had worked steadily and completed his tasks in five days. When his level of commitment was being judged, the fact that Chris was the only group member staying on schedule seemed to go unnoticed. The lesson that somebody like Chris would take away is that getting ahead in corporate life is looking as busy as possible. A true cynic would spend half their day holding a stack of papers with a cell phone to their head, walking laps around the office, making sure to walk by the manager's door. A specific example in this exercise comes from George Costanza, who realizes in an episode of *Seinfeld* that his bosses believe him to be a great worker merely because his car is broken down in the parking lot, which they mistake for him coming in early and leaving late.

The 18 people in this book who lived lives of enormous productivity understood the fault in this logic. They did not confuse efficiency with effectiveness, as modern managers often do. Efficiency is performing a task in the best possible manner with the least waste of time, even if the task itself is useless. A farmer, for example, walks through his field and hand plants his seeds with the fewest number of steps and hand movements necessary. He is pleased with himself at the end of the day for all his hard work. But effectiveness means performing a set of actions adequate to accomplish a purpose, producing the intended result. It is a vague concept concerned with achieving goals. Another farmer doesn't bother with manually planting seeds; he uses a 15-row John Deere Planter to seed his field in $1/1000^{th}$ of the time. He is pleased with himself for preparing such a massive harvest. Effectiveness is about doing the right things, while efficiency is about doing things right.

The conclusion of Elsbach's study notes that most workers are concerned with efficiency. They wonder how to do repetitive tasks faster and better in order to get more of them done. They are obsessed with numbers and sum totals. But because efficiency is a measurable concept – like hours worked in a week – it is a lazy metric to determine work output. Few ask if what they are doing is worth doing in the first place. Doing a job well means nothing if the job itself is meaningless. A sales team might be tasked with making 70 calls a day. They decide to go above and beyond and clock in 80 or 90 calls. But what if none of those calls convert into a sale? What is the purpose of clocking in more calls if it does not accomplish its task?

The misguided quest for efficiency is best illustrated in America's obsession for higher international test scores among its middle and high school students. In December 2013, Secretary of Education Arne Duncan announced that once again American students were falling terribly behind students in 61 other countries in Asia and Europe. He released the latest international assessment of performance scores in reading, science, and mathematics. China led the nations of the world in all three categories.

But are his worries justified? Are Chinese schools really producing super students who will control the global economy? Not exactly. The Chinese school system is perhaps the best example of a model that praises efficiency and ignores effectiveness. According to Yong Zhao, author of *Who's Afraid of the Big Bad Dragon? Why China Has the Best (and Worst) Education System in the World*, China has the best education system in the world because of its high international test scores. But it has the worst education system because those test scores come from rote memorization and sacrificing originality, individualism, and creativity. China follows a Confucian system of education that is thousands of years old and values rote learning. This system was designed to maintain Chinese civilization by requiring knowledge of Eastern philosophy.

This learning system's pernicious effects has filtered out into the rest of the economy and drained China's technology sectors of their effectiveness. The government rewards the production of patents for new products, even though most of these patents are worthless. A high percentage of them are junk or only demonstrate small cleverness. Many are fraudulent. High school students are given extra points for college admission if they receive patents for their proposals. As a result, many patents read like an American high schooler's essay on *The Great Gatsby*. Zhao even mentions a school where a ninth-grade class had received over 20 patents; even middle school students had collected national patents. A billion-dollar shadow industry is devoted to writing these papers to sell to students and professionals who cannot write their own.

This broken incentive system ruins a scientist's ability to conduct original research. According to Zheng Yefu, a professor at Peking University and the author of the 2013 book *The Pathology of Chinese Education*:

> No one, after 12 years of Chinese education, has any chance to receive a Nobel Prize, even if he or she went to Harvard, Yale, Oxford or Cambridge for college... Out of the one billion people who have been educated in Mainland China since 1949, there has been no Nobel Prize winner... This forcefully testifies [to] the power of education in destroying creativity on behalf of the [Chinese] society.

If slavish attention to efficiency doesn't work, then what does? Researchers have spent over a century trying to formulate a scientific approach to the difference between efficiency and effectiveness. The best theory was put forward by – surprisingly – an Italian gardener/economist over 100 years ago. In the early 1900s University of Lausanne Professor Vilfredo Pareto noticed that in his garden 80% of his peas were produced by 20% of the pea pods. He realized this division appeared in other areas of life. He created a mathematical formula to demonstrate unequal income distribution in Italy. Pareto showed that over 80 percent of the land was owned by 20 percent of the population. He found that a similar distribution existed in other countries.

Pareto's principle, or the 80/20 rule, has migrated out of economics and into other fields, particularly business management. Project managers claim that 20 percent of their work takes up 80 percent of their time. Likewise, 20 percent of their sales force makes 80 percent of the company's sales; 20 percent of the staff causes 80 percent of problems; and 20 percent of the stock takes up 80 percent of the warehouse space. To give even more examples of the Pareto Principle in the field of quality control, 80 percent of process defects come from 20 percent of process issues; 80 percent of delays arise from 20 percent of possible delays; and 80 percent of customer complaints come from 20 percent of products or services.

This principle suggests that nobody should mistake long hours of work as an end in and of itself. Forget the dictum that hard work is its own reward. Those that take this belief to its absurd extreme could end up like Japan's salarymen, who die of *karoshi*, or "death by overwork." This term became legally recognized as a cause of death in the 1980s as Japan's economy boomed and educated workers spent an obscene number of hours chained to their office desks. Health professionals observed that employees could not work 12 or more hours a day for 6-7 days a week without serious health repercussions. Salarymen died from heart attacks or strokes due to stress. *Karoshi* became such a widespread problem in Japan that politicians introduced penalties against companies who brought it about. If *karoshi* was considered the cause of death, surviving family members could claim government compensation and up to $1 million from the company in damages.

The International Labour Organization noted one case of *karoshi* in which an employee at a major snack food processing company worked 110 hours a week (over 15 hours a day). He died from a heart attack at the age of 34. Another employee of a large printing company worked over 4,300 hours a year and died from a stroke at the age of 58. A 22-year-old nurse died from a heart attack after 34 hours of continuous work five times a month.

The Economist relates a story of Kenichi Uchino, a third-generation Toyota employee, who died of *karoshi* at the age of 30 in 2002, collapsing at 4 am at work, after more than six months with a work-week minimum of 80 hours. "The moment when I am happiest is when I can sleep," he told his wife the week of his death. As a manager of quality control, he was constantly training workers, writing reports, and attending meetings when not on the production line. Toyota treated all his time off the production line as unpaid yet necessary to his job. So did a Japanese court, which ruled that long hours were integral part of his job and that Toyota did nothing wrong in the way it treated him. The government did not appeal against the verdict.

Japanese workers officially only work 1,780 hours a year, slightly under America's 1,800 hours. But that does not take into account the "free overtime" of several extra hours a week completing job tasks, or weekend training sessions that go unpaid. Many Japanese workers maintain a punishing schedule as part of the labor culture. Staffers want to hold onto their lifetime employment benefits and feel obligated to work long hours lest their position becomes temporary. Hard work is also considered a cornerstone of Japan's rise from the wreckage of World War II onto its perch at the top of the global economy. The notion of self-sacrifice puts group interests above individual interests.

These workplace problems have compounded since the beginning of the global recession in 2009. At companies that laid off employees, those that remain have to complete their former colleagues' tasks along with their current duties. Even if they are not busy, they stay long after hours in order not to appear expendable. It is for these suspected reasons that Japan's suicide rate consistently hovers above 30,000 a year, more than double the rate of the U.S. According to one government survey, nearly 90 percent of workers claim they did not know what a work-life balance meant.

Ironically, a *karoshi*-style of work does not lead to results. The 18 figures in this book would look upon a Japanese salaryman with a mixture of confusion and pity. They all strove for effectiveness above efficiency. They gladly dropped any habits or tasks that prevented them from reaching their higher goals in life and ruthlessly cut away what was not important. Benjamin Franklin proudly pruned away branches of his life that did not bear fruit. He cut habits and friendships out of his life that wasted an inordinate amount of time. Thomas Aquinas and Isaac Newton rejected schmoozing with aristocrats, which was an integral part of medieval and early modern social advancement, in favor of focusing on their studies. Julius Caesar and Justinian gladly offloaded tasks that they did not have to personally perform in order to tend to the needs of their empires. Philip II was slightly less adept at delegation, getting bogged down in the minutiae of his far-flung colonies, but he still set up a sophisticated administration system that let the realms of Spain largely govern themselves.

The figures in this book reached such high levels of effectiveness due to their commitment to excellence. Productivity was never an accident in their lives. It came about as a result of intelligent planning, focused effort, and commitment to goals higher than their own aggrandizement. They realized that time was their most precious commodity, even more precious than money, because it could never be reclaimed. Napoleon considered the loss of time to be irretrievable in war because operations go wrong through delays. He knew that battles progressed according to many factors outside his control, and he could not create more time. He was once asked during a battle by a marshal for more time to maneuver his unit and carry out his part of the attack. Napoleon responded, "You can ask me for anything you like, except time."

Most of all they lived out the philosophy of Orthodox Rabbi Menachem Mendel Schneerson, the last Lubavitcher Rebbe and one of the most influential Jewish leaders of the 20th century. He transformed an insular Hasidic group, which nearly went extinct with the Holocaust, into one of the most influential forces in world Jewry. Schneerson understood how to take a small thing and transform it into something influential and powerful.

His words describe all those who did far more with their time on earth than anyone else in history: "When you waste a moment, you have killed it in a sense, squandering an irreplaceable opportunity. But when you use the moment properly, filling it with purpose and productivity, it lives on forever."

BIBLIOGRAPHY

"Archimedes The Super Villain." *Classical Wisdom Weekly*. July 28, 2014.

Asimov, Isaac. *I. Asimov: A Memoir*. Reprint edition. New York: Bantam, 1995.

"Avicenna | Biography - Persian Philosopher and Scientist." *Encyclopedia Britannica*.

Bacharach, Samuel B. "Stop Procrastinating: 5 Tips From Ben Franklin." *Inc.com*. January 31, 2013.

Bell, Peter N. *Social Conflict in the Age of Justinian: Its Nature, Management, and Mediation*. Oxford University Press, 2013.

Blanco, Sebastian. "In Deep with Tesla CEO Elon Musk: Financials, Falcon Doors and Finding Faults in the Model S." *Autoblog*. September 7, 2012.

Bram, Marvin. *The Recovery of the West*. Xlibris Corporation, 2002.

Bramly, Serge, and Leonardo Da Vinci. *Leonardo: The Artist and the Man*. Translated by Sian Reynolds. London; New York: Penguin Books, 1995.

Brassfield, Marissa. "Inside the Daily Routine of Elon Musk." *Ridiculously Efficient | Superhuman Productivity*. November 25, 2014.

Buelow, George J. *A History of Baroque Music.* Indiana University Press, 2004.

Chatfield, Anthony. "Productivity Hacks of 8 Famous Thinkers and Leaders." *Lifehack.* Accessed February 5, 2015.

Chesterton, G. K. *St. Thomas Aquinas.* Courier Corporation, 2009.

Clear, James. "The Physics of Productivity: Newton's Laws of Getting Stuff Done." *Lifehacker.* September 30, 2014.

Coren, Stanley. *Sleep Thieves.* New York: Free Press, 1997.

Cox, Simon. *Decoding The Lost Symbol: The Unauthorized Expert Guide to the Facts Behind the Fiction.* Simon and Schuster, 2009.

Davis, Lauren. "Science Fiction Novelists Reveal Their Daily Writing Routines." *Io9.* December 10, 2008.

Dobbs, B. J. T. *The Foundations of Newton's Alchemy.* CUP Archive, 1983.

Emmerson, Richard K. *Key Figures in Medieval Europe: An Encyclopedia.* Routledge, 2013.

Franklin, Benjamin. *The Autobiography of Benjamin Franklin.* New edition. New York: Dover Publications, 1996.

Freeman, Philip. *Julius Caesar.* Reprint edition. Simon & Schuster, 2008.

Gelzer, Mattias. *Caesar: Politician and Statesman*. Translated by Peter Needham. Cambridge, Mass.: Harvard University Press, 1968.

"Georg Philipp Telemann (1681-1767), Composer of the Week - BBC Radio 3." *BBC*. Accessed February 5, 2015.

Glick, Thomas F., Steven Livesey, and Faith Wallis. *Medieval Science Technology and Medicine: An Encyclopedia*. Routledge, 2014.

Goldsworthy, Adrian. *Caesar: Life of a Colossus*. 1 edition. Yale University Press, 2006.

Harmon, Franchee. *Making Purpose Work: The Challenge of Growing Ourselves and Our Companies*. HPH Publishing, 2006.

Hasan, Heather. *Archimedes: The Father of Mathematics*. The Rosen Publishing Group, 2006.

Heath, Peter. *Allegory and Philosophy in Avicenna (Ibn Sina): With a Translation of the Book of the Prophet Muhammad's Ascent to Heaven*. University of Pennsylvania Press, 2010.

Hendry, Erica. "7 Epic Fails Brought to You By the Genius Mind of Thomas Edison." *Smithsonian*. November 20, 2013.

Herd, Van Alan. *The Theology of Sir Isaac Newton*. ProQuest, 2008.

Hyman, Arthur, James J. Walsh, and Thomas Williams. *Philosophy in the Middle Ages (Third Edition): The Christian, Islamic, and Jewish Traditions*. Hackett Publishing, 2010.

Israel, Paul. *Edison: A Life of Invention*. 1st edition. New York: John Wiley & Sons, 2000.

"Jobs for Life: Death by Overwork in Japan." *The Economist*, December 19, 2007.

Jonnes, Jill. *Empires of Light: Edison, Tesla, Westinghouse, and the Race to Electrify the World*. 9.12.2004 edition. New York: Random House Trade Paperbacks, 2004.

Josephson, Matthew. *Edison: A Biography*. 1 edition. New York: Wiley, 1992.

Khan, Muhammad Mojlum. *The Muslim 100: The Lives, Thoughts and Achievements of the Most Influential Muslims in History*. Kube Publishing Ltd, 2009.

Kihn, Heinrich. *Exegesis and Empire in the Early Byzantine Mediterranean: Junillus Africanus and the Instituta Regularia Divinae Legis*. Mohr Siebeck, 2003.

Lasswell, Harold Dwight. *Power and Personality*. Transaction Publishers, 2009.

Lovett, A. W. *Philip II and Mateo Vázquez de Leca: The Government of Spain (1572-1592)*. Librairie Droz, 1977.

Maas, James B., Megan L. Wherry, David J. Axelrod, Barbara R. Hogan, and Jennifer Bloomin. *Power Sleep: The Revolutionary Program That Prepares Your Mind for Peak*

Performance. 1st edition. New York: William Morrow Paperbacks, 1998.

Magill, Frank N. *The Middle Ages: Dictionary of World Biography.* Routledge, 2012.

Malik, Tariq. "4 Tips for Business Success From Entrepreneur Elon Musk." *Business News Daily.* August 2, 2010.

Marshall, Taylor. "Top Five Productivity Tips from Thomas Aquinas [Podcast]." January 25, 2014.

Marshall, Taylor. *Thomas Aquinas in 50 Pages: A Quick Layman's Guide to Thomism.* Saint John Press, 2013.

Masters, David. "Writing Secrets of Prolific Authors." *Write to Done.* Accessed February 1, 2015.

McGinnis, Jon. *Avicenna.* Oxford; New York: Oxford University Press, 2010.

McLynn, Frank. *Napoleon: A Biography.* New York: Arcade Publishing, 2002.

Meier, Christian. *Caesar: A Biography.* Basic Books, 2008.

Millard, Candice. *The River of Doubt: Theodore Roosevelt's Darkest Journey.* 1st edition. Anchor, 2009.

Moore, Ray. "'Most Prolific' Composer: It's Not Bach." *UALR Public Radio: News & Culture for Arkansas*, July 24, 2013.

Morris, Edmund. *The Rise of Theodore Roosevelt*. Reprint edition. Modern Library, 2010.

Nicholl, Charles. *Leonardo Da Vinci: Flights of the Mind*. Reprint edition. New York, N.Y.: Penguin Books, 2005.

Northrop, Henry Davenport, and Charles Haddon Spurgeon. *Life and Works of Rev. Charles H. Spurgeon: Being a Graphic Account of the Greatest Preacher of Modern Time*, 1892.

Parker, Geoffrey. *Imprudent King: A New Life of Philip II*. Yale University Press, 2014.

Parker, Geoffrey. *The Grand Strategy of Philip II*. New Haven Conn.: Yale University Press, 2000.

Pevsner, Jonathan. "Leonardo Da Vinci, Neuroscientist." *Scientific American* 23, No. 1 (January 2014).

Pickover, Clifford. *Archimedes to Hawking: Laws of Science and the Great Minds Behind Them*. Oxford University Press, 2008.

Popova, Maria. "19-Year-Old Isaac Newton's List of Sins." *Brain Pickings*. Accessed February 5, 2015.

Ravitch, Diane, Ian Johnson, Andrew Delbanco, and Diane Ravitch. "The Myth of Chinese Super Schools." *The New York Review of Books*, November 20, 2014.

Renick, Timothy Mark. *Aquinas for Armchair Theologians*. Westminster John Knox Press, 2002.

Roberts, Andrew. *Napoleon: A Life*. Viking Adult, 2014.

Roosevelt, Theodore. *Theodore Roosevelt; an Autobiography*, n.d.

Rosen, William. *Justinian's Flea: Plague, Empire and the Birth of Europe*. Random House, 2010.

Rothstein, Edward. "Telemann and the Canary Cantata." *The New York Times*, February 27, 1981.

Schmenner, Roger W. *Getting and Staying Productive: Applying Swift, Even Flow to Practice*. Cambridge University Press, 2012.

Sertillanges, A. G. *Thomas Aquinas: Scholar, Poet, Mystic, Saint*. Sophia Institute Press, 2011.

Spurgeon, Charles. *The Autobiography of Charles H. Spurgeon Compiled from His Diary, Letters: And Records by His Wife and His Private Secretary [Rev. W.J. Harrald]*. American Baptist Publication Society, 1892.

Spurgeon, Charles. "Warnings Against Laziness," in *Metropolitan Tabernacle Pulpit: Containing Sermons Preached and Revised by C. H. Spurgeon, during the Year 1862, Vol. VIII*. London: Passmore and Alabaster, 1863.

Starr, S. Frederick. "Moderate Islam? Look to Central Asia." *The New York Times*, February 26, 2014.

Spurgeon, Charles. "Warnings Against Laziness," in *Metropolitan Tabernacle Pulpit: Containing Sermons Preached and Revised by C. H. Spurgeon, during the Year 1862, Vol. VIII.* London: Passmore and Alabaster, 1863.

Swain, Joseph P. *Historical Dictionary of Baroque Music.* Scarecrow Press, 2013.

Tate, Carson. *Work Simply: Embracing the Power of Your Personal Productivity Style.* Penguin, 2015.

Thordarson, Bob. "Benjamin Franklin's 7 Best Productivity Tips." *Scrubly Blog. How-To Tech and Productivity.* Accessed February 5, 2015.

Torrell, Jean-Pierre. *Saint Thomas Aquinas: The Person and His Work.* CUA Press, 2005.

Wawrykow, Joseph Peter. *The Westminster Handbook to Thomas Aquinas.* Westminster John Knox Press, 2005.

White, George Savage. *Memoir of Samuel Slater: The Father of American Manufactures.* s.n., 1836.

Wisniewski, J. "Leonardo Da Vinci Was An Incredible Procrastinator." *KnowledgeNuts.* January 23, 2014.

ALSO BY MICHAEL RANK

TURN THE PAGE
TO READ AN EXCERPT

CHAPTER TEN

GEORGE KOVAL (1913-2006)
THE SOVIET SPY FROM SIOUX CITY, IOWA

Vladimir Putin, a former KGB officer who spent the 1980s in East Germany recruiting foreigners and sending them undercover to the United States, had a soft spot in his heart for sleeper agents. It was little surprise that on November 2, 2007, he honored a recently deceased Cold War deep-cover agent with a gold star, designating him a Hero of the Russian Federation, the nation's highest civilian honor. The ceremony introduced George Koval to the world.

But it was a great surprise to his friends and family. Russian acquaintances knew Koval as a physics professor, whose career was long and respectable but unremarkable. Americans knew him as a native Iowan – his actual birthplace – educated in Manhattan and a World War II veteran who loved baseball. He was affable, athletic, and a genius in technical studies. Once Vladimir Putin blew his cover – hidden for decades in old KGB files and only recently recovered by historians – both Russians and Americans learned his true identity as a man at the top of the pantheon of Soviet spies. His reconnaissance efforts were so far-reaching that they revised decades of the narrative of Cold War espionage.

George Koval worked at the Manhattan Project's laboratories in Oak Ridge, Tennessee, and Dayton, Ohio. He was the only Soviet agent to gain access to the top-secret project. Putin credited him with securing classified intelligence on the most crucial aspect of the atomic bomb, the device that initiates the nuclear reaction. The nuclear secrets he stole reduced by years the time it took for Russia to develop nuclear weapons, thus ensuring the preservation of its strategic parity with the United States, which it achieved in 1949. If not for him, four decades of the U.S.-Soviet arms race would have never happened.

Koval took these secrets to the grave, but bits of his legacy were first revealed in a 2002 book by Russian historian Vladimir Lota, entitled *The GRU and the Atom Bomb*. It recounts the activities of a Soviet spy code-named Delmar who, only with the exception of British scientist Klaus Fuchs, did more than anyone else in developing the Soviet atomic weapons program. His activities were so well hidden that Putin is thought to have only learned of them in 2006 when he saw Koval's portrait at a GRU museum and asked of the man's identity. The answer shocked the Russian premier.

George Abramovich Koval was born in Sioux City, Iowa, on Christmas Day in 1913. He was the second of three sons to a family of Jewish immigrants from Belarus, at the time part of the Russian Empire. The city had a large Jewish population and at least a half-dozen synagogues. At the turn of the century it appeared poised to become another Chicago, a Midwestern cultural and commercial hub that attracted immigrants from across the world. His parents came to Sioux City as part of a massive wave of Russian and Eastern European immigrants to the United States in the late nineteenth and early twentieth centuries, particularly its Jewish citizens, who suffered under Russia's pogroms. Many came to Iowa for its farms, meatpacking plants, and coal mines. The Koval family spoke Belarusian in the home, a language closely related to Russian, but Koval retained an American tinge in his fluent Russian for the rest of his life.

His father, Abraham, a carpenter, and his mother, Ethel, the daughter of a rabbi and former member of an underground Russian revolutionary socialist group, were ardent communists and supported the Bolshevik Revolution. They believed a new regime would right the wrongs of the anti-Semitic tsarist Russia and remained in contact with family members in the newly-formed Soviet Union. Abraham participated in local communist organizations, which flourished in pre-World War II America. In early 1914, the leftist Industrial Workers of the World organized a "free speech fight" in Sioux City to add industrial and agricultural laborers to their union. They found sympathy among newly arrived immigrants such as the Kovals, who were prone to exploitation by employers. In 1924, Abraham became the secretary of the Sioux City branch of ICOR (derived from the Yiddish name, *"Idishe Kolizatzie in Sovetn Farband"*), an organization that sought to establish a Jewish agricultural settlement in the Soviet Union. ICOR's goal was to construct the autonomous region in the Soviet Far Eastern province of Birobidzhan. The plans succeeded, and in 1934 it became the capital of the Jewish Autonomous Republic.

George Koval's Midwestern boyhood made him an ideal "sleeper" or deep-cover agent. By all appearances he was a typical American. Koval played baseball and spoke fluent American English, fully comfortable in the conservative social mores of early twentieth-century rural Iowa. Yet his bilingualism and biculturalism made him a spy in the classic mold of Jack Higgins's Kurt Steiner in *The Eagle Has Landed*, a novel about a German-English spy attempting to kidnap Winston Churchill during World War II. In the story, as Grosjean recounts, Steiner's father is a major general in the German army and his mother an American. The bicultural child becomes the leader of a German commando unit. Having been brought up in both England and Germany, he is the perfect candidate to abduct the prime minister.

Koval did not perform such daring feats in his spy career, but he came from a similar background. The youth was American by upbringing, Russian by family, and communist by indoctrination in his early years. He became involved in the communist cause, joining a local chapter of the Communist League, which in the years prior to the Cold War had not yet received pariah status. Classmates remembered Koval as being vocal about his communist beliefs. He was a delegate for the Young Communist League at the 1930 Communist Party in Iowa Convention when he was still sixteen. In

1931, he was arrested for occupying a municipal office and demanding shelter for two women evicted from their homes.

Koval was also exceptionally bright. He graduated from Central High School at age fifteen as a member of the Honor Society He enrolled in the University of Iowa to study electrical engineering for two and a half years.

According to his FBI file, he commented to his schoolmates that his family planned to return to Russia in 1932. ICOR facilitated their move to Birobidzhan in the midst of the Great Depression to work on a collective farm, a "utopia" that Russia was building for the Jews. The region was an isolated province in the Russian Far East near the Chinese border. Stalin established it in the 1920s to integrate Jews into Soviet society and protect them from the anti-Semitism of the Russian gentile population while also creating a buffer against Chinese and Japanese expansion. To the Kovals, it was a new beginning for Russia, free from its tsarist past and Jewish pogroms. While on the farm, Koval improved his Russian enough to study chemical engineering in Moscow at the Mendeleev Institute of Chemical Technology. He met Lyudmila Ivanova while at the Institute, whom he married shortly after. He graduated in 1939 with honors and became a Soviet citizen.

It is unknown when Koval began to work for the Soviet secret service (GRU), but he was drafted into the army shortly after graduation. The GRU was likely scouting universities across the Soviet Union, looking for intelligent students with potential for a career in espionage. Several years of Stalin's purges depleted the ranks of the intelligence community, and there were many open positions. Koval was perfect for this role. He was raised as an American and could pass as one with little difficulty. He possessed a knowledge of science – a highly valued attribute at a time when Russia wanted to develop its military capabilities against increasing Nazi aggression – which made it possible for him to infiltrate laboratories in America. Yet he was a doctrinaire communist, a true believer in the cause, and would likely not defect to the West if embedded there, a perennial problem for the Soviet Union throughout the Cold War, when spies abandoned their posts for the greener pastures of Europe or America.

Koval was "drafted" into the Soviet Army in 1939 to cover up his disappearance from Moscow. Exactly how he was recruited is unclear, but Koval has written that he did not accept an offer of military training. He never wore a uniform nor was sworn into the armed forces. Rather, he was trained by the GRU to conduct espionage in the United States for an eight-year term, from 1940 to 1948.

Koval found it easy to sneak back into America even though his parents had relinquished their U.S. passports. In October 1940, he boarded a U.S.-bound tanker. Upon arrival in San Francisco, he simply walked across through border control with the ship's captain, his wife, and little daughter, who sailed together with him. He immediately went to New York. There he took command of the GRU station.

The Raven Electric Company, which supplied a number of U.S. firms such as General Electric, served as the station's cover. He created a cover story so bland that it would stifle the interest of any listener: He was an unmarried orphan raised by his aunt, and he never traveled. Koval kept his political opinions to himself, never uttered a word about the Soviet Union, and established no contact with any communists outside of his handlers. It worked: After only a few months in the U.S., Koval registered for the draft. Raven secured for him a job deferment for a year because his Soviet handlers believed that his ability to steal information on chemical weapons would be compromised if he were drafted. They could not have been more wrong.

He joined the army on February 4, 1943. Koval received his basic training at Fort Dix before being sent to the Citadel in Charleston, South Carolina, to join the 3410th Specialized Training and Reassignment Unit. On August 11 he became a member of the Army Specialized Training Program (ASTP). This program gave talented enlisted men technical training at colleges and universities. Koval was enrolled in City College of New York (CCNY) to further develop his knowledge of electrical engineering. It was considered a Harvard for the poor and famous for brilliant students. He excelled there.

"He was very friendly, compassionate and very smart. He never did his homework," said Arnold Kramish, a retired physicist who studied with Koval at City College and later worked with him on the Manhattan Project, in an interview with *The New York Times* following Koval's death. "Of course, that was because he was already a college graduate back in Moscow, although we didn't know that at the time."

Koval's classmates thought it strange that he was a decade older than them. Although he fit in well with the group of student-soldiers, and he was something of a father figure, many aspects of him stood out. He smoked his cigarettes down to where they almost burned his fingers, which Kramish later learned was a distinctive Eastern European habit. He was quite a ladies' man, although his classmates didn't know that he had a wife in the Soviet Union. He had a casual manner, standing six feet tall, with a penetrating gaze.

The Army Specialized Training Program ended shortly after Koval enrolled due to the Allied need for more combat troops. Most program participants were transferred to the infantry. Koval, however, received a spy's chance of a lifetime. The Manhattan Project suffered manpower shortages and requested technically adept recruits from the Army. A colleague of his, Duane Weise, believed that Koval's high scores on the Army's intelligence test and his specialized training in handling radioactive materials caught their attention. Koval was sent to the blandly-named Special Engineer Detachment, which was actually a branch of the nuclear project.

The Manhattan Project was America's most secret military endeavor. In order to produce fissile materials, it grew during the war to employ more than 130,000 and cost over $2 billion ($26 billion in 2014). Los Alamos devised the bomb, but Koval was sent to the Oak Ridge laboratories, a critical research center where the bomb's parts and fuel were developed. It was considered the most difficult part of the atomic project.

His job in Oak Ridge couldn't have been better for his spy mission if his Soviet officers had wished it into existence. He was an army sergeant given the position of "health physics officer," requiring him to track radiation levels throughout the complex. Koval was given top-secret clearance and access to the entire facility. He drove from building to building, making sure stray radiation did not harm the workers. The Soviet Union now had a trained operative inside a secret center producing America's most closely guarded military technology. He was even given his own Jeep, which very few officers had.

"He didn't have a Russian accent. He spoke fluent English, American English. His credentials were perfect," said Steward Bloom, senior physicist at the Lawrence Livermore National Laboratory in California, who studied with Koval and called him a regular guy who "played baseball and played it well," usually as a shortstop.

"I saw him staring off in the distance and thinking about something else. Now I think I know what it was."

Koval's spy career spanned World War II and the Cold War, a period that ushered in the high-water mark of global espionage. All Cold War powers developed at least one government agency dedicated to intelligence gathering. The CIA was formed in 1947, and its goals were shaped at the outset by America's foreign policy challenges. It was authorized to conduct "secret operations against hostile foreign states or groups or in support of friendly foreign states or groups." In response, Russia formed the KGB in 1954, which acted as the internal security, intelligence, and secret police. Within U.S. borders, the FBI prosecuted spies, which it did with fervent zeal between 1935 and 1972 – the years of director J. Edgar Hoover, a fanatical anti-communist. It began investigating Soviet espionage in 1943 and doubled in size to 13,000 agents within two years. The agency scored many early victories against Soviet moles, particularly when it received information from Elizabeth Bentley, who prior to her capture passed on intelligence to Russia. She gave them a 112-page confession, naming 80 people as spies or paid informants.

Koval was aware of the growing paranoia of Soviet infiltration. He took many precautions, and sent information to his GRU handler through the use of couriers and the diplomatic pouch from the Soviet Embassy. He likely used other means that still remain unknown due to the limited number of extant sources that describe his manner of espionage.

Manhattan Project scientists developed two types of atomic bombs, one based on a relatively simple technology that required an enriched form of uranium, the other based on plutonium, which had not been isolated until 1941. Scientists at Oak Ridge discovered that in order to build a functional plutonium warhead, they required enriched uranium and the rare element polonium to initialize the chain reaction. Both materials produced lethal levels of radiation. Strict safety protocol was required, and Koval continually monitored radiation levels throughout the complex. He also kept inventory of experimental substances that were tested for their effectiveness as bomb fuels.

In his reports to Moscow, he described the Oak Ridge complex and its functions, the production of polonium and uranium, and the monthly volume of polonium. He notified them that polonium was being sent to Los Alamos. The Soviets already had a spy there, Klaus Fuchs, who gave the Soviets detailed information about the bombs. The information supplied by Fuchs and Koval on the importance of polonium allowed the Soviets to integrate the leaked scientific secrets coming from the two labs.

Koval was not the only agent who spied on the Manhattan Project for the Soviets. In recent years, as Russian archives have opened to historians and classified FBI files from decades back have been declassified, scholars and federal agents have identified at least a half-dozen Soviet spies involved in the project. They were mostly concentrated at Los Alamos. But all of these were "walk-ins," or spies who were ideological sympathizers but lacked rigorous training. Koval, in contrast, was an intelligence officer who had been groomed for his assignment in the Soviet Union for years and had wider access to America's atomic plants than any other mole.

On June 27, 1945, Koval was transferred to another secret lab in Dayton, Ohio, where the polonium initiator was being constructed and the polonium itself refined. The factories refined polonium 210, a highly radioactive material. It was crucial, as plutonium was considered too unstable to initiate a successful atomic reaction. Once again, Koval's status as health physics officer gave him free rein throughout the installation. He was there to witness scientific breakthroughs and the ultimate triumph of a controlled nuclear explosion. The initiator was a success, and the first atomic bomb was detonated at Trinity in New Mexico on July 16 (the experiment in which Los Alamos director Robert Oppenheimer, watching the terrible mushroom cloud form, quoted the Bhagavad-Gita: "Now I am become death, the destroyer of worlds.") Three weeks later, in

August 1945, two bombs, one uranium-based and the other plutonium-based, were detonated over Hiroshima and Nagasaki, forcing Japanese Emperor Hirohito to surrender.

After the detonation of the two bombs, the Soviet Union accelerated its nuclear program. The information provided by Koval and other spies pushed their program forward by years. They rapidly developed the polonium initiator for the plutonium bomb. This initiator was based on the information provided by the Soviet agent Delma– the code name for George Koval. In 1946, the CIA believed that the Soviets would not be able to successfully build an atomic bomb until 1950 at the earliest or 1953 at the latest. Their estimates tilted toward 1953. They were shocked when intelligence reports revealed that Soviets had tested a plutonium-based atomic bomb on August 29, 1949, at their Semipalatinsk Test Site in Kazakhstan.

In the run-up to the Soviet nuclear triumph, Koval was offered continued classified work in Dayton but began to fear his cover would be blown. Another GRU officer, Igor Gouzenko, had defected to Canada and revealed the extent of Soviet infiltration into the United States, even within the Manhattan Project. Another scientist, Alan Nunn May, was arrested in Britain as a result of Gouzenko's confession. At no point was Koval's cover in danger of falling apart; his alibi was airtight. But worries remained. Michael Sulick argues that he fled due to danger, because the Soviet Union would not have recalled him otherwise due to his excellent placement. The Soviets held on tenaciously to their spies; in the case of atomic spy David Greenglass, his handlers redirected him to the University of Chicago to target scientists working on classified military research even after he had been discharged from the U.S. Army and lost access. Therefore, Koval would not have left the United States unless capture was imminent.

Andrey Shitov, a Russian chronicler of Koval, writes that a Soviet defector told the FBI that an unknown GRU chief was based in New York and dealt electronic products. American counterintelligence agents found old Soviet literature that hailed the Koval family as happy immigrants from the United States. A pamphlet read that the Kovals came to the Soviet Union and "had exchanged the uncertainty of life as small storekeepers in Sioux City for a worry-free existence for themselves and their children."

Intercepted Soviet intelligence cables had begun to implicate KGB-run spies such as Harry Dexter White, a senior Treasury Department official in the Roosevelt administration who died of a heart attack before being subpoenaed in 1948. Koval's old colleagues in Oak Ridge and Dayton confirmed that they had been interviewed by the FBI in 1949 and 1950. They were asked specifically about Koval, whom they learned at this time was not an orphan but an Iowan with communist parents. The FBI finally understood the full extent of their failure but swore his fellow scientists to secrecy. The U.S. Government refused to admit this failure, as it would have been highly embarrassing to have this divulged.

But they were too late for damage control. Koval had already left America, and his departure had been planned for years. Following the end of World War II, Koval received his honorable discharge from the army with reference to his "brilliant" work. He earned two medals, one "For Victory in World War II." Koval returned to New York, where he resumed his studies again at City College He completed his bachelor's degree on February 1, 1948, graduating *cum laude*. He then told his associates that he received a job offer to plan the construction of a power plant in Europe. Koval obtained a new U.S. passport for six months' travel and used a trading company, Atlas Trading, as a cover for his travel plans. He boarded the ocean liner *SS America* for Le Havre in October 1948, departing American shores. Koval never returned.

Meanwhile, the arms race between America and the Soviet Union that Koval launched began in earnest. As Michael Walsh recounts in *The Smithsonian*, when reports reached Harry Truman in 1949 that the Soviets had detonated a nuclear weapon, he apprised the American public of their test on September 24: "We have evidence that within recent weeks an atomic explosion occurred in the USSR. Ever since atomic energy was first released by man, the eventual development of this new force by other nations was to be expected. This probability has always been taken into account by us." But behind these resolute words, policy makers, government officials, and scientists debated whether to push for international arms control or produce the next generation of nuclear weapons. Truman made the decision when he authorized the development of the hydrogen bomb in 1950. Fears of nuclear annihilation between the world's superpowers were more real than ever.

Koval delivered intelligence to the Soviets that advanced their military technology by years, to the point that they were nipping at the heels of the United States in the decades-long arms race of the Cold War. Despite his achievements, Koval was not particularly well received in his adopted homeland. Whether due to Soviet embarrassment that they had to steal military secrets to develop their nuclear program rather than rely on their own scientific finesse, or worries that Koval could be an American double agent or mole, the intelligence establishment kept him at arm's length. He did not receive any high awards when he arrived, and his background as a spy in America negatively affected his life.

When he was discharged from the Soviet Army in 1949, he was given the rank of private and described as an untrained rifleman, despite nine years of service in the armed forces. This apparent poor performance in the army as well as Koval's academic and foreign background hindered his ability to find a job. He sought a position as a teacher or researcher but suspicions about him lingered. According to his CV, he spent 10 years, from 1939 to 1949, as an enlisted soldier but received no promotion despite his decade of service and higher education. Koval ended up having to beg the GRU to help him find a job.

He was only able to secure a position as a laboratory assistant at the Mendeleev Institute following Stalin's death in 1953, when his old superiors intervened with the Ministry of Higher Education. He earned his doctorate there and became a professor and prolific scientist, publishing over 100 scientific papers in the next four decades. His students thought him unexceptional, but they sometimes giggled when he pronounced the Russian words for technical terms such as "thermocouple" in an American accent. Koval worked as an instructor for the next 40 years. Rossiiskaia Gazeta said that he was a soccer fanatic even when elderly people at the stadium who knew of his secret past as a spy would quietly point him out.

Back in the United States, security tightened down and the Red Scare flared up. Accusations of Soviet espionage by former communist spies had been made public. These included testimonies by Elizabeth Bentley and Whittaker Chambers, a former Communist Party USA member and Soviet spy who later renounced communism and fiercely criticized it. He testified before the House Committee on Un-American Activities (HUAC) in the perjury and espionage trial of Alger Hiss, an American government official accused of being a Soviet spy in 1948 and convicted of perjury in relation to this charge in 1950. American intelligence officials deciphered coded messages that unearthed an increasing number of Soviet spies. The FBI and CIA and its allies broke up Soviet spy rings in the years ahead, most notably the Cambridge Five. This ring consisted of British communists recruited during their education at Cambridge University in the 1930s. They passed on information to the Soviets during World War II and into the 1950s until fleeing Britain. The extent to which the establishment had been infiltrated was only now becoming apparent.

Koval lived for decades in obscurity, unknown in America or by his compatriots. Only in 2000 did the GRU recognize his accomplishments when it threw him a closed ceremony at its headquarters. He was awarded a medal for his service to military intelligence. The story of his exploits began leaking to the Russian media, but he was still only known by his code name. Koval himself preferred it this way. When Vladimir Lota interviewed him for his book, *The GRU and the Atom Bomb*, Lota wanted to identify Delmar by his true name, but the retired spy refused. He even kept his true identity from his family. They had vague knowledge that he worked for the GRU and that it was somehow related to the nuclear bomb, but for him it was a forbidden topic. Perhaps he was scared that he would be seen as a liability to the Soviets and shipped off to prison camp. "Maybe I should not complain (and I am not complaining – just describing how things were in the Soviet Union at the time) but be thankful I did not find myself in a Gulag, as might well have happened." Koval eventually changed his mind, but he died a month later on January 31, 2006, in Moscow at the age of 92.

In the decade before his death, Koval's old American army friend, Arnold Kramish, tried to reestablish contact with him, even after learning from an FBI interview that he had been a spy. As Walsh notes, Kramish came across some references to Koval and the Mendeleev Chemical institute in 2000 while at the National Archives.

Kramish contacted the Moscow institute and was surprised to hear his old friend answer on the other end of the line. "It was an emotional moment for both of us," he said. Kramish and Koval began a letter correspondence that turned into swapping e-mails. Koval did not go into great details of his life, but he lamented that the Soviet Union did not offer him any high awards upon his return, especially amid "the terrible government-instigated-and-carried-out anti-Semitic campaign, which was at its peak in the early fifties."

Public appreciation only came posthumously, and even this came with an asterisk. First, Putin's acknowledgement in 2007 of Koval's contributions had less to do with honoring him and more to do with politics. The award ceremony came a month before Russian Parliamentary elections and coincided with Putin's promise to restore Russia's military might. Second, nations rarely bring public attention to their spies, even long after they have died, and particularly in the paranoid, secretive world of Russian espionage. It was likely to do with what Sulick describes in *Spying in America* as Putin touting the past achievements of the intelligence services as part of his nationalist agenda. As the former leader of the Federal Security Service (*Federal-naya Sluzhba Bezopasnosti*), he has significantly increased the authority, budget, and morale of Russia's intelligence services and grafted them into his personal power apparatus, blackmailing and spying on his political opponents.

Few spies have done so much for their homeland but received so little recognition. But in an odd twist, Koval's understated legacy is further credit to his ability as a spy. The American-born communist never sought out a career in espionage, he only saw it as the best means to support the communist cause. He never had any regrets and truly believed in the system. This is perhaps the greatest asset for a spy to have: to be content with a job well done, even if the public never knows of his accomplishments – as Joshua's spies realized over 3,000 years ago. After all, if his job is done correctly, they never will.

END OF THIS EXCERPT

ENJOYED THE PREVIEW?

BUY NOW

OTHER BOOKS BY MICHAEL RANK

Off the Edge of the Map: Marco Polo, Captain Cook, and 9 Other Travelers and Explorers That Pushed the Boundaries of the Known World

Lost Civilizations: 10 Societies that Vanished Without a Trace

The Most Powerful Women in the Middle Ages: Queens, Saints, and Viking Slayers: From Empress Theodora to Elizabeth of Tudor

History's Greatest Generals: 10 Commanders Who Conquered Empires, Revolutionized Warfare, and Changed History Forever

From Muhammad to Burj Khalifa: A Crash Course in 2,000 Years of Middle East History

History's Most Insane Rulers: Lunatics, Eccentrics, and Megalomaniacs from Emperor Caligula to Kim Jong-Il

The Crusades and the Soldiers of the Cross: The 10 Most Important Crusaders, From German Emperors to Charismatic Hermits and Warrior Lepers

Greek Gods and Goddesses Gone Wild: Bad Behavior and Divine Excess, From Zeus's Philandering to Dionysus's Benders

History's Worst Dictators: A Short Guide to the Most Brutal Rulers, From Emperor Nero to Ivan the Terrible

How Iowa Conquered the World: The Story of One Small Farm State's Rise to Global Dominance

ABOUT THE AUTHOR

Michael Rank is a doctoral candidate in Middle East history. He has studied Turkish, Arabic, Persian, Armenian, and French but can still pull out a backwater Midwestern accent if need be. He also worked as a journalist in Istanbul for nearly a decade and reported on religion and human rights.

He is the author of the #1 Amazon best-seller "From Muhammed to Burj Khalifa: A Crash Course in 2,000 Years of Middle East History," and "History's Worst Dictators: A Short Guide to the Most Brutal Leaders, From Emperor Nero to Ivan the Terrible."

ONE LAST THING

If you enjoyed this book, I would be grateful if you leave a review on Amazon. Your feedback allows me to improve current and future projects.

To leave a review please go to the book's Amazon page. Thanks again for your support!

42740903R00147

Made in the USA
San Bernardino, CA
08 December 2016